The Ghosts of
HAMLET

The Ghosts of
HAMLET
The play and modern writers

Martin Scofield

CAMBRIDGE UNIVERSITY PRESS
CAMBRIDGE
LONDON   NEW YORK   NEW ROCHELLE
MELBOURNE   SYDNEY

Published by the Press Syndicate of the University of Cambridge
The Pitt Building, Trumpington Street, Cambridge CB2 1RP
32 East 57th Street, New York, NY 10022, USA
296 Beaconsfield Parade, Middle Park, Melbourne 3206, Australia

First published 1980

Printed in Great Britain at the
University Press, Cambridge

Library of Congress Cataloguing in Publication Data
Scofield, Martin.
The ghosts of Hamlet.
Includes index.
1. Shakespeare, William, 1564–1616. Hamlet.
2. Shakespeare, William, 1564–1616—Influence.
3. Literature, Modern—20th century—History and
criticism. I. Title.
PR2807.S38   822.3′3   79-21297
ISBN 0 521 22735 6

To Lyn

—Who's there?
—Nay, answer me. Stand and unfold yourself   *Hamlet*, I.i

—Do you see yonder cloud that's almost in shape of a camel?
—By th' mass and 'tis, like a camel indeed.
—Methinks it is like a weasel.
—It is backed like a weasel.
—Or like a whale.
—Very like a whale.   *Hamlet*, III.ii

Contents

Acknowledgements

My debts to former critics are many, but I hope they will be found to be gratefully acknowledged in the course of this study. Here, I would like to thank my wife, Lyn Innes, and the following friends and colleagues, who have either read and commented on parts of the first draft or made suggestions for reading: David Ellis, Edward Greenwood, Derek Marsh, Howard Mills, and Marion O'Connor; also Roger Cardinal, who helped me in elucidating and interpreting parts of Mallarmé. I would also like to thank the staff of the Cambridge University Press for their help throughout the various stages. Finally, I am indebted to Mrs Freda Vincent for her invaluable help with typing.

PART 1

Modern writers and the ghosts of *Hamlet*

Introduction: *Hamlet*, criticism and creation

Hamlet is a specular and ductile medium: it has reflected its readers and been used as material by other writers. Everyone 'knows the story', but not only do countless critics differ as to its interpretation, there is also fundamental disagreement about what happens in it. As a result the play has become a critical ocean

> where each kind
> Does straight its own resemblance find.

Hamlet says that the purpose of playing is 'to hold a mirror up to nature', and the play has done this in a special sense, for it is a mirror in which every man has seen his own face. Hamlet also says (half changing the metaphor) that the mirror will show 'the very age and body of the time, his form and pressure'; and like a piece of wax the play has either taken the impress of the age which has interpreted it, or been moulded into other forms.

This quality presents a particular challenge to criticism. There do not seem to have been any critical theories which have fundamentally replaced Arnold's dictum, that the aim of criticism is 'to see the object as in itself it really is'. But what is *Hamlet* 'really', if different ages and different critics within each age have seen it so differently? One answer might be that the differences are not always so great as they seem. A reader might still find much in Coleridge's or in Bradley's account of the play without in the end agreeing with his view of what is the centre of interest. This seems to be a necessary attitude to take to criticism, or we are in danger of thinking we have exhausted the value of a great critic just because we feel his main idea about a play to be unsatisfactory. Another answer which is sometimes given is that since all critical positions are 'relative' there is no one 'right' interpretation of a work of literature, and that we should give up looking for such an interpretation and be content with a plurality of readings. But this seems unsatisfactory, and contrary both to the natural desire of the reader and the experience of criticism.

What I, the reader, want to achieve is an understanding of *Hamlet*. If I am presented with various views I want to know how they are related to each other, and which is to have prime place in my experience of the play. What do I experience when I read or see *Hamlet*? It is a question which seeks, ultimately, a single answer: *this* is what I have experienced. We ask criticism to help us place ourselves in the fullest relation to the work in question. But our sense of it must be ours, must be subjective. This is a truism but is still forgotten. It is also still confused with the idea that there can be no shared standards or readings. On the one hand there is the sentiment of the casual reader, 'Well this is what *I* think, and that's enough for me.' On the other there is what one might call the Olympian-professorial view: 'There are many plausible readings. Let us entertain as many as possible without committing ourselves to any of them.' Both these attitudes seem equally inadequate. The first denies the possibility of deepening our understanding by means of criticism. The second abandons the necessary subjectivity of the genuine reader, and the aim at defining and agreeing on a reading that best establishes the view of one's own age. Arnold's 'object as in itself it really is' must remain the aim, tantalizing, unobtainable perhaps in a full scientific sense (i.e. provable, demonstrably true or false) but attainable in the limited sense that a particular age may achieve a predominant view of the object.

But with *Hamlet* more than with any of Shakespeare's plays the 'object' has almost completely disappeared in our time. The text is there, refined and analysed: though even the text is disputed, and two 'good' versions and an earlier makeshift version have to be considered before we can really be sure what object to look at, let alone describe or interpret. Beyond this, the object in the sense of what we agree to look at as the play, with commonly seen outlines and masses, light and shade, is something of a blur. In performance, where we expect selection and emphasis, we have often received renderings without a guiding idea, or else emphases personal to the

4

point of idiosyncrasy. The only common denominator is the lowest: the play is enjoyed, if at all, as a revenge melodrama with some famous philosophizing tacked on.

The last coherent and generally accepted view was probably Coleridge's; this persists to some extent in our own time. But of the best-known counter-Coleridgean views of this century there is probably not one that has commanded general assent. T. S. Eliot, Salvador de Madariaga, G. Wilson Knight, L. C. Knights: three or four names spring readily to mind of critics who have added something to our sense of the play. In so far as one can readily estimate these things, Wilson Knight's essay would seem to have had more general influence than any of the others. His first essay in *The Wheel of Fire*, with its strong emphasis on Hamlet's morbidity and paralysing consciousness of death, is an extreme counter-Romantic view. It has aroused 'orthodox' rejoinders, but the elements of the play which it isolates are perhaps now felt to be *in* the play and part of our experience of it. But it is significant that Wilson Knight felt the need to add two reconsiderations of the play. Like him, perhaps, we cannot feel that his first essay is an account of the whole play: we cannot forget so easily the healthier side of Hamlet's sense of life, his free disinterested enthusiasm for the players, his admiration for Horatio, and the possibility (if no more than that) of his love for Ophelia. Nor does Wilson Knight's view deal with the problem of what we are to make of the Ghost, or settle how exactly we should see Claudius.

There is not yet, then, a shared modern sense of the play. There are signs that first-hand critical thinking about the play is still going on, which may more freshly and firmly define our sense of it, and I shall attempt to draw on some of these in Part 2 of this study, a reading of the play. But for the reader and playgoer who is still looking for 'sight-lines' on the play there is one avenue which is still relatively unexplored – that of the response to *Hamlet* in modern creative literature, or of what one might call the image of *Hamlet*.

A number of the most important writers of the late nineteenth and early twentieth centuries have employed this image. It exists where Hamlet the character, or *Hamlet* the play, is taken up by a creative writer and used as a *persona*, or myth, or symbol in the writers' own creations. The unique malleability or indeterminate nature of the play almost invites this: it seems to leave room for further creation. Eliot noted this fact as a danger for criticism and sought to exclude it from his own; but he finely availed himself of it in his poetry. The play has seemed for these writers to be a kind of symbol for a certain type of experience, but one which is not clearly defined. When we ask of the play 'Who's there?' it challenges us to stand and unfold ourselves. Modern literature in the broad sense of the term seems unique in this: it has found in *Hamlet* as no previous literature has done a special stimulus and symbol. The enigmatic character of the hero and the different perspectives it is possible to take of the play as a whole have made them themes for reflection and symbols for the perplexing, fragmented experience of modern life. The ghosts of *Hamlet* haunt the imagination of modern writers and bid them 'Remember me', providing them with both a standard and a riddle.

Criticism and creation are both involved in this response. On one hand the writers have all been in varying degrees concerned with what the play means in itself: on the other they have drawn on it in the constructions of their own imaginations. The following study has therefore two related aims. One is to look at the 'image' of *Hamlet* in the imaginative creations, the criticism, and sometimes just the passing allusions and references, of six writers who I hope it will be agreed can broadly be called modern: Mallarmé, Laforgue, Eliot, Joyce, Lawrence and Kafka. As a kind of postscript to Chapter 1 on Mallarmé I have added a briefer chapter on some observations of Claudel and Valéry which continue the Mallarméan themes. And I have added a further writer, Kierkegaard, who, although he wrote in the mid nineteenth century, seems in spirit and even more in terms of his influence on thought to be characteristically modern, and is related interestingly to Kafka's view of *Hamlet*. By shining a particular kind of lamp on the works of these writers we may hope to illuminate certain features in a new way; to show what, in relation to their response to *Hamlet*, they have in common with one another and where they differ. To look at their response to the play will be a way of highlighting qualities of their thought and imagination. Secondly, this investigation should throw light back on to the play itself. In the work of these creative writers we may begin

6

to discover features of a modern sense of the play which is not entirely present in the tradition of modern criticism. The investigation and conclusions will necessarily be tentative. It is a question of seeing what aspects of the play the modern creative mind has been most concerned with, and from these to begin to formulate certain features common to the different responses. No single 'view' can be expected to emerge, but elements which might help to construct that view will be discernible.

Sometimes, then (as in the chapters on Laforgue and Joyce), this study will become more absorbed in the works of the writers themselves and how Shakespeare's play works itself into their primary creations, and plays its part in their achievement. In other chapters (e.g. on Claudel and Valéry, and on Kierkegaard), their ideas will be used as starting-points for developing thoughts about the play. In the case of Kafka, a remark in his diaries about the play leads to a comparison of the world of *Hamlet* with the real and fictional worlds of Kafka. The present book can be seen as a study of tradition in the sense in which Eliot used the word: of the way in which a past work of art helps to form the art of the present and is in turn 'changed' by it. The chapters can be read as separate essays on each writer, but they are intended to be held together by this main preoccupation.

There is one group of modern writers, who have made of Hamlet a symbol in their own art, with whom this study might be expected to deal. They are the twentieth-century Russian poets, particularly Pasternak and Akhmatova. I have not included them partly because of the difficulty of getting a real sense of their poetry in translation; but mainly because their response to *Hamlet* still seems to be what could be called romantic rather than modern. Hamlet for them is still the isolated romantic hero pitted against society, through whose mask they look at the world. Pasternak's poem 'Hamlet' uses the character as a *persona* through whom the poet speaks of his sense of fate, of being caught up in both the drama of his personal life and the larger drama of history.

> The noise is stilled. I come out on to the stage.
> Leaning against the doorpost
> I try to guess from the distant echo
> What is to happen in my lifetime.

Modern writers and the ghosts of *Hamlet*

> The darkness of night is aimed at me
> Along the sights of a thousand opera glasses
> Abba, Father, if it be possible,
> Let this cup pass from me.[1]

What I have called its romanticism is summed up in the line 'I am alone; all drowns in the Pharisees' hypocrisy.' Akhmatova puts on the mask of Ophelia, and in 'Reading Hamlet' uses the prince to evoke a sense of heroism which contrasts with her own implied weaknesses.[2] In some ways Turgenyev's response to Hamlet sixty or so years earlier is less romantic than that of the later writers. In the story 'A Hamlet of the Schtigri district' he presents a garrulous failure who talks through the night of his romantic yearnings and his actual failures, his cultivated mind and his profound unoriginality. He is to be associated with Turgenyev's view of Hamlet in his essay 'Hamlet and Don Quixote', where the two are contrasted as at the opposite poles of heroism, and Turgenyev urges that Russia needs more of the latter type, reckless and idealistic, and less of the Hamlet-like philosophical dreaminess. Turgenyev is closer to someone like Laforgue in this view of Shakespeare's figure: but still there is not the suggestion of the radically divided and ambiguous figure of the French symbolists, or of Kafka, or of the modern English writers I shall consider. Turgenyev essentially only pushes the romantic Hamlet of Coleridge or of Goethe just over the edge of comedy, by associating the figure with the 'superfluous man' of his day. And of course in doing this he was primarily satirizing the vogue for the melancholy 'Hamlet' posture among Russian young men, rather than offering a reading of the play itself.

Yeats, too, has some interesting things to say about *Hamlet* in his prose writing; and brings Hamlet into at least two poems. But this study will not discuss him in detail since his view of the play and character is still what could be called a primarily romantic one: he does not, it seems to me, share the distinctively modern concern with the play which characterizes the writers under consideration. For much of his life his sense of Hamlet was derived from the deep impression on him of Henry Irving's performance, which his father took him to see when he was ten or twelve. 'For many years Hamlet was an image of heroic self-possession for the poses of youth and childhood to copy, a combatant of the battle within myself.'³ His Hamlet, together with Byron, was a source of heroic poses. Later on he saw Hamlet as the type of the intellectual, 'the wavering, lean image of hungry speculation', but still also the heroic swordsman with 'agile rapier and dagger' between his fingers (p. 142). His sense of Hamlet's spirituality was more intense in a diary entry of 1909, in which he wrote: 'I feel in *Hamlet*, as so often in Shakespeare, that I am in the presence of a soul lingering on the stormbeaten threshold of sanctity. Has not that threshold always been terrible, crime-haunted?' (p. 522). But it is still a view that may very much, I think, be called romantic. Curiously enough this idea of Hamlet's approach to sanctity has a parallel in Pasternak's poem 'Hamlet', where the speaker uses the words of Christ in Gethsemane, 'Abba, Father, if it be possible, / Let this cup pass from me.' In neither writer is there the sense of Hamlet's radically divided nature, his uncertain perception, or his sense of a fundamentally ambiguous paternal authority, which, I hope to show, are characteristic of the modern views of *Hamlet* I propose to explore. Nor do the two late references to Hamlet in Yeats's *Last Poems* seriously qualify the sketch I have given. In 'Lapis Lazuli' Hamlet's tragic gaiety is not distinguished from that of Lear, Ophelia and Cordelia – that is, from the gaiety of the tragic hero in general. The idea of 'Gaiety transfiguring all that dread' could, perhaps, be more easily applied to Hamlet than to the other characters Yeats mentions, but I confess the idea seems to me a difficult one. Certainly I think that most of the writers examined in these pages would have found it difficult to think of Hamlet's 'dread' as so easily transfigured by 'gaiety' at the end of the play. Finally, the reference in 'The Statues' to 'No Hamlet thin from eating flies' again seems to return to the Coleridgean Hamlet, the Hamlet who feeds on the impalpable air of ideas: he typifies, in this poem, Western reason and intellect as opposed to Asiatic sensuality. Yeats's Hamlet is undoubtedly interesting, but it does not associate itself with the nexus of problems which I think is more or less common to the writers explored in this book.

It would have been possible to conclude this study with the reflection that *Hamlet* is a play which prompts different writers to very different kinds of response and interpretation, and that it resists any attempt to find in it a single meaning. But while it would be foolish to be dogmatic about an individual reading, it still seems the natural aim of criticism to want to reach a particular way of seeing, that which is most broadly satisfying to the critic himself and which seems to him to contain what is central to the play. It cannot, of course, be satisfying in any real way if it is uninformed, or merely idiosyncratic, or unaware of other, different responses to the play. But it can also hardly be satisfying to leave a number of different, often conflicting views in suspension in one's mind, as if they were all equally valid and every part of them equally suggestive. If his ideas are going to be of any interest to anyone else, a critic must doubtless be asking a broader question than simply 'What does this mean to me?' But if he is not also asking that question, the question 'What has this meant to others?' will be rootless and uninteresting, and the final question, 'What should this mean to anyone?', cannot be asked.

Part 2 of this study, then, consists of a reading of the play in the light of certain ideas that, I think, predominate in the responses of the modern authors examined earlier. I had been struck by some of these ideas, particularly that of authority, and had explored them in the play, before I undertook the studies of the modern writers. The connections with Kafka were the first to interest me, and it is still, I think, the influence of Kafka that is uppermost in my reading of the play. If it is objected that I may have approached the modern writers with certain already formed ideas about the play, and have therefore been led to find what I was looking for, I must partly submit to that objection. But I would also claim that the elements I describe of the writers' relations to the play are features of their works and minds, and not simply imposed by me. Whether, with the writers and with the play, I have succeeded in identifying things that are really there, or, in Arnold's sobering phrase,* have simply aired my own psychology, I must leave the reader to judge.

1

'Bounded in a nutshell . . . king of infinite space'
Stéphane Mallarmé

Mallarmé made Hamlet a symbol of himself as poet, and *Hamlet* a symbol of poetry. Hamlet is cited by name in one poem, 'Le Pitre Châtié'; in at least two others he is there implicitly, unnamed, and in a new guise; and in two prose essays Mallarmé addresses himself to the meaning of the play. In all this the view of Hamlet can be summed up as follows: he epitomizes the problem of the opposition in life of the ideal and the real; of contemplation and action; of essence and existence. He is called upon to act, but action is a false compromise. In his soul he is noble, but in the exigencies of his existence he is evil. He also epitomizes the preoccupation that is behind all Mallarmé's work, the preoccupation with impotence – more specifically, with the inability to realize or to become the true self, or, for the artist, the inability to create, to add to the life of the race. For Mallarmé, the drama of *Hamlet* is an interior drama, fought out in the protagonist's mind. He is the symbol of the poet, whose duty is to the Ideal, but who must 'make', and in making compromise the purity of that Ideal. As a criticism of *Hamlet* this is immediately, perhaps, open to objections; but we are concerned with it as an example of the 'creative use' of the play in mask or mythification. The interest will lie primarily in what poetic use Mallarmé makes of the mask and the myth. But if we trace its effect in his art we may find that it contributes something of value also in relation to the play.

What seems to be Mallarmé's first reference to *Hamlet* in his writing comes in a letter to Cazalis in 1862. He compares himself to Hamlet, but to a 'ridiculous Hamlet':

How disillusioned you will be when you see this peevish individual who spends whole days without thinking, his head resting on the marble chimney-piece: a ridiculous Hamlet who cannot explain his weakness.[1]

11

It is not perhaps entirely clear whether Mallarmé sees Shakespeare's Hamlet as 'ridiculous' here, or whether it is simply he who makes a 'ridiculous Hamlet'. The idea may be simply of the absurdity of *posing* as Hamlet, or an idea that there is something absurd in Hamlet himself. The distinction is obviously important, but, whichever is the case here, the two categories will always tend to overlap. The parody will always tend to leave some traces on the original, and the most successful parody is always a permanent criticism of the original. Hamlet had already been seen in parodic fashion by Baudelaire in his poem 'La Béatrice'. The poet sees his melancholy self, complaining to nature and 'sharpening the dagger of his thought on his breast', tormented by a group of demons who mock him as a *poseur*:

> "Contemplons à loisir cette caricature
> Et cette ombre d'Hamlet imitant sa posture,
> Le regard indécis et les cheveux au vent.
> N'est-ce pas grand' pitié de voir ce bon vivant,
> Ce gueux, cet histrion en vacances, ce drôle,
> Parce qu'il sait jouer artistement son rôle,
> Vouloir intéresser au chant de ses douleurs
> Les aigles, les grillons, les ruisseaux et les fleurs,
> Et même a nous, auteurs de ces vieilles rubriques,
> Réciter en hurlant ses tirades publiques?"[2]

The poet would have turned his head away but for the fact that he saw 'the queen of my heart' among the crowd of demons. They see him as a parody of Hamlet (the Hamlet, perhaps, of a romantic actor like Rouvière). But the cumulative effect of this kind of poetic treatment is to modify our sense of Hamlet himself, in the end. If the character is often associated with the *poseur*, there is a tendency to see him as something of a *poseur* himself (an idea which can certainly be substantiated in a number of places in Shakespeare's text). The tendency is continued in Laforgue, and reaches a kind of climax in the identification, made though finally rejected, by Eliot's Prufrock. For all Baudelaire's interest in *Hamlet*, and for all the parallels which have been pointed out between his own predicament and Hamlet's,[3] the example above appears to be the only time that Baudelaire mentions the character in his poems. When he writes on Delacroix's engravings and paintings of Hamlet it is the melancholy sensitivity of the hero which he comments on rather than his heroism.[4] Delacroix's vision of the character makes him seem peculiarly effete: the engraving of his meeting with the Ghost shows a fastidious, shrinking figure, a 'beautiful, ineffectual angel' like Arnold's Shelley, not the powerful figure of Shakespeare's imagination at that moment, whose

> fate cries out
> And makes each petty artere in this body
> As hardy as the Nemean lion's nerve.   (I.iv. 81–3)

Delacroix's Hamlet is like (perhaps partly derives from) Goethe's, the fine and costly vase which is shattered by the great oak tree (Hamlet's task) planted in it. Such a character lends itself to parody, and Baudelaire's imagination responded to it particularly in this way.

Mallarmé begins by taking up the same strain. In his early sonnet 'Le Pitre Châtié', written in 1864, Hamlet is used as an epithet for the clown, recalling Baudelaire's 'this pauper, this actor on holiday, this queer fish'. But the poem is complex and needs to be examined in full, for it shows Mallarmé's earliest fashioning of the Hamlet mask, a fashioning that eludes any simple formulation.

> Yeux, lacs avec ma simple ivresse de renaître
> Autre que l'histrion qui du geste évoquais
> Comme plume la suie ignoble des quinquets,
> J'ai troué dans le mur de toile une fenêtre.
>
> De ma jambe et des bras limpide nageur traître,
> A bonds multipliés, reniant le mauvais
> Hamlet! c'est comme si dans l'onde j'innovais
> Mille sépulcres pour y vierge disparaître.
>
> Hilare or de cymbale à des poings irrité,
> Tout à coup le soleil frappe la nudité
> Qui pure s'exhala de ma fraîcheur de nacre,
>
> Rance nuit de la peau quand sur moi vous passiez,
> Ne sachant pas, ingrat! que c'était tout mon sacre,
> Ce fard noyé dans l'eau perfide des glaciers.[5]   (p. 31)

Broadly the poem is about an attempt to break out of the clown's role, and to make a bid to achieve the life of the Ideal. This life could be seen as a life of love – the poet begins with an invocation to 'eyes'.

13

But this aspect is emphasized more in an earlier version of the poem. There, the 'lakes' are 'plantés de beaux cils qu'un matin bleu pénètre' and the symbolism suggested by the eyes is maintained throughout the sonnet. Here the eyes, though emphatically placed at the beginning so that we do not entirely forget them, become at once 'lakes', and it is into a lake that the clown plunges in his desire to be reborn. 'Ivresse' immediately sets up a warning note: the feeling of escape is exultant but drunken; and the note is continued in the next four lines. 'Limpide nageur traître' has two conflicting adjectives: 'limpide' suggesting openness and honesty as well as the suggestion of the swimmer in the clear water, and 'traître' which counteracts this with suggestions of betrayal and deceit. 'De ma jambe' adds a grotesque note – the swimmer seems to be one-legged. 'Bonds multipliés' is odd too: 'bounds' or 'leaps' are not the natural movement of a swimmer, and suggest a confusion of elements. And this feeling of strangeness is continued into the next lines where the movement becomes a kind of burrowing one, a digging of 'mille sépulcres'. There is a double feeling of escape and entrapment, of rebirth and death, which concludes in the phrase 'pour y vierge disparaître'. The attainment of purity is confused by the sense of a possibly perverse withdrawal from life.

In the sestet this double feeling is continued. The sense of purity mingles with the feeling of loss and punishment. 'Hilare or de cymbale à des poings irrité' recalls the cymbals of the clown's circus in an image of slightly frenetic merriment: the freshness of nature still seems to contain elements of his previous suffering. Thus too the sun's striking the clown's nakedness is felt as a kind of punishment.

The last three lines are difficult, mainly because of punctuation and syntax. At first reading the 'Rance nuit de la peau' seems to come as something that follows 'le soleil' of the previous three lines. But the verb 'passiez' is in the past imperfect tense so it would seem to indicate a time before the present of 'frappe' of two lines previously. 'Ingrat' again seems at first to refer to the 'rance nuit', but it must in fact refer to the speaker. The general sense of the last three lines would therefore run: 'When you were passing over me, rancid night of the skin, I didn't know, ungrateful as I was, that it was my whole consecration, this greasepaint . . .'. This reading is

Stéphane Mallarmé

supported by the last three lines of the earlier version of the poem, which carry just this general sense:

> Ne sachant pas, hélas! quand s'en allait sur l'eau
> Le suif de mes cheveux et le fard de ma peau,
> Muse, que cette crasse était tout le génie. (p. 1416)

The idea, then, is that in plunging into the lake the clown washes off the greasepaint of his profession; in abstract terms, in choosing the life of the Ideal or of Love, he loses the protective covering of his role, which was his 'genius'. Edmond Bonniot criticized Mallarmé for writing 'Le génie' in the first version, as if this clown's role were characteristic of all genius and not just his. Mallarmé seems to have accepted this criticism by writing 'mon sacre', 'my consecration', in the final version. This is how one of Mallarmé's critics, Wallace Fowlie, reads the poem.[6] 'Le fard' is 'mon sacre', as it was 'le génie' in the earlier version.

The main element that the second version of the poem adds to the first is the symbol of Hamlet. The clown 'evoking with his gestures as with a pen the soot of the stage-lamps' is Hamlet, and also the writer Mallarmé, who evokes this poem with his pen. The French word plume can also of course mean the English 'plume' or 'feather', which would be appropriate for the clown, and which also has a significant topical association with the figure of Hamlet on the stage, particularly in the performance of Mounet-Sully about which Mallarmé wrote (see below, pp. 25–6). The plume in the cap was an essential prop in the contemporary stage picture of Hamlet, and Mallarmé refers to it in his essay of 1886, where he also quotes some lines of Banville: 'Le vent qui fait voler ta plume noire / Et te caresse, Hamlet, ô jeune Hamlet!'[7] The plume in Mallarmé also has a range of other associations – angelic, luciferian, Promethean; with reason and with hesitation or oscillation – which might be interesting to ponder in relation to Hamlet but for which there is not the space here.[8] The association with Hamlet is also important in 'Un Coup de Dés (see below, pp. 27–8). Hamlet is the 'doubter' (Mallarmé's description from his later note on 'Hamlet and Fortinbras'),[9] the buffoon, who cannot act. He withholds his love from Ophelia and ends by saying he never loved her. He is the type of impotence. This Hamlet is renounced for decisive action, for the

15

clown's leap, or the writer's writing of the poem. But the action is punished. The purifying waters are also treacherous; the sun strikes the clown in a kind of ritual punishment. Shakespeare's Hamlet says

> O that this too too solid flesh would melt,
> Thaw, and resolve itself into a dew,   (I.ii. 129–30)[10]

and the lines seem to be echoed and implicitly criticized in the poem. The 'rance nuit de la peau' does dissolve into the waters of the lake. The flesh melts away, but with it all genius and humanity. The poem, while making Hamlet its own symbol, suggests to us certain reflections on the play, the main one being concerned with the destructiveness and anti-humanity of Hamlet's idealism. The other reflections are on Hamlet's clownishness and his element of the histrionic. He seems to need this protective clothing. In stripping it away and acting with effect (murdering Polonius and sending Rosencrantz and Guildenstern to their deaths) he seems to lose some of his humanity. His hatred of this too too solid flesh comes to seem something close to a hatred of life. Hamlet thinks of man ideally as a god. But his flesh-hatred entangles him in toils of inhumanity and moral hysteria. His excessive revulsion against the flesh kills Ophelia. He too renounces 'le mauvais Hamlet' in a sense – in his decisive action against the courtiers and his return from the journey to England. But another kind of evil seems to overtake him, and he goes to his death with everything ill about his heart.

The poem embodies the dilemma of having to live in a real world while longing (as Mallarmé did) for the Ideal. Even to write is to be involved in the 'suie ignoble des quinquets', yet only in writing can the Ideal be realized. Utterly to reject the clown's or writer's role is to reject his humanity, without which he cannot live. Mankind cannot bear very much ideality.

In *Igitur*, written in 1869, Mallarmé attempts a complex metaphysical drama which enacts his struggle with the problem of 'chance' ('le hasard') and creative action. It seems always to have been associated with *Hamlet*, most notably by Paul Claudel in his essay 'Le Catastrophe d'Igitur' of 1926.[11] According to George Moore, Mallarmé once talked of writing a play entitled *Hamlet et le Vent*, about 'a young man, the last of his race, living in an isolated castle, haunted by the howling of the wind, at a loss to know whether it urges him to wait or act'.[12] If this may be credited it provides another link between *Hamlet* and *Igitur*. But the work is so complex and obscure that it would be best to begin with a short attempt at a summary.

It is an inner drama – Mallarmé said it was to be imagined in the reader's own mind – and not meant for performance. At one point Mallarmé makes fun of conventional notions of stage heroism, when Igitur's decisive action is to descend a staircase 'in place of descending on to the stage on horseback'. There is one character, the young prince, and a few mysterious 'props': a staircase, a book of magic, a clock, the statue of a chimera, a mirror, a window with thick curtains, arrases on the walls, some dice: items which suggest, I think, the furnishings of the nineteenth-century poet's room. More mysterious and less locatable in an actual scene, there is also a tomb with double doors. There are five 'acts': I. 'Le Minuit', II. 'Il Quitte la Chambre et se perd dans les escaliers', III. 'Vie d'Igitur', IV. 'Le Coup de Dés', V. 'Il se Couche au Tombeau'. In so far as is possible – for the process of the drama is one of a mingling of ideas and objects, a shifting inner movement of the spirit – the 'action' can be summarized as follows:

I. *Le Minuit.* We are to imagine the 'presence' of midnight – not one moment in time, but subsisting. Time is associated with 'the dream', 'a rich and useless survival', also with the furnishings of the room, particularly with the 'hangings' or 'arrases', and with an opened book on the table. These things are the paraphernalia of time, the cluttered objects of a closed room, barring the hero from action. Time is the enemy of eternity, but, as in Eliot, only through time is time conquered. In the clock there is a jewel, 'the only survival and jewel of eternal night', which seems to symbolize this Eternity. At the end of the 'act', Time speaks to the Night: 'Farewell, night that I was, your proper tomb; but who, the surviving shadow, will change into Eternity.'

II. *Il Quitte la Chambre.* Night is left listening to the faint echo of Time. The sound of time is extinguished but another sound persists. Then only the sound of beating wings is heard. This represents 'not some final doubt of the self' but 'the familiar and continued beating of a superior age, the many geniuses of which were anxious to collect all its secular dust into its sepulchre in order to see itself

17

reflected in a proper self'. This 'age' sees itself in its apparitions: 'nebulous science' on one hand, and a volume with an heraldic clasp on the other. And the sound of this age 'is nothing, I know, but the absurd prolongation of the noise of the closing of the tomb door which the entrance to this stairwell recalls'.

The hero is then faced with a tomb with double doors. One is associated with science and the past, the other with magic and the future. Behind and before these doors the 'infinite lie' continues, 'the shadows of all my apparitions', massive in the emptiness 'in which I hear the beatings of my own heart'. The hero does not like the sound. The perfection of his certainty hinders him. 'All is too clear.' 'I would like to re-enter my former uncreated shadow and strip away by thought the disguise, which necessity has imposed on me, of living in the heart of my race.'

Which of the two doors should he choose, since there is no future represented by either by them? Are they not both merely his reflection? Must he still fear chance, 'which divided me into shadows and created time'? Is not chance annulled by the end of time? There is a whispering sound, and the same beating and rustling sounds as before, but this time they are the sounds of his former self, his *personnage* and his duality. Now he feels his former self separating away from him: he is going to 'dissolve into myself'.

In the mirror the figure of the *personnage* disappears and the mirror is left in its purity.

III. *Vie d'Igitur*. 'I have always lived with my soul concentrated on the clock' – so that the moment it strikes should remain forever, and be 'my pasture and my life'.

Now Igitur's position is summed up: 'The complete past of his race which weighs on him in a sensation of the finite, the hour of the clock precipitating this "ennui" in heavy, stifling time, and his waiting the accomplishment of the future, form pure time, or "ennui", rendered unstable by the malady of ideality.' Igitur looks in the mirror and sees himself disappearing; around him there is an absence of atmosphere, and the pieces of furniture seem to be 'twisting their chimeras in the emptiness, the curtains shuddering invisibly, anxious'. He opens up the furniture of the room and empties out its mystery, the unknown, its memory, silence, human faculties and impressions. And when he believes he has become

18

himself again he concentrates his soul on the clock, whose time disappears in the mirror or flees in the curtains, too completely, not even leaving him to the 'ennui' which he implores and dreams.

Now 'he separates himself from indefinite time and is!' His reflection in the mirror gradually disappears: he dares to uncover his eyes and watch the process, sees the figure disappearing into eternity and becoming 'the horror of eternity', nourishing itself on the supreme shudders of the chimeras and the instability of the arrases, until it detaches itself from the glass which is left absolutely pure; while the furnishings, curtains and the rest (all the attributes of finite time) fall 'into an attitude which they would keep for ever'.

IV. *Le Coup de Dés*. 'But the action is accomplished.' His Self is manifested because he takes up madness: he 'admits the Act and voluntarily recaptures the Idea, as Idea'. And because the Act denied the power of chance he concludes that the Idea was part of necessity. It was madness to admit the Act absolutely, but the madness was necessary because it denied the power of chance. 'All that he amounts to is the fact that his race has been pure, that it has drawn from the Absolute its purity in order to be the Absolute, and in order to leave of it only an Idea in turn culminating in Necessity: and that as for the Act, it is perfectly absurd, except as a (personal) movement rendered up to the Infinite: but so that the Infinite is at last *fixed*.'

Igitur shakes the dice before going to join the ashes of his ancestors. He closes the book, blows out the candle with the breath which contains chance, and, crossing his arms, lies down on the ashes. 'The Absolute has disappeared into the purity of his race ... – Immemorial race, whose time which weighed heavy has fallen, excessive, into the past, and who, heavy with chance, has only lived for its future. – Once chance has been denied with the help of an anachronism, a *personnage*, supreme incarnation of his race, feeling in himself, thanks to the Absurd, the existence of the Absolute, has in his solitude forgotten the human word in the book of magic and the thought in a flame, the one announcing this negation of chance, the other illuminating the dream he is in. The *personnage* who, believing in the existence of the sole Absolute, imagines himself everywhere in a dream (he acts from the Absolute point of view), finds the act useless, for there is and there is not chance – he reduces chance to the *Infinite* – which, he says, must exist somewhere.'

I have translated this passage as clearly and literally as possible, but it may still seem especially obscure, even for Mallarmé. I therefore offer a gloss: Igitur's ancestors and the tradition in which he is involved have fallen away into the past; Igitur has forgotten traditional learning and thought (those of the *grimoire* or Black Book and of the 'luminary'), and has acted purely on his own impulse to conquer chance. He cannot destroy or deny the element of chance in life by decisive action (this was his earlier mistake); but he can act in a way that recognizes the agency of chance in Time, but its absence in the 'dimension' of Eternity or the Absolute. This is why Mallarmé writes: 'There is, and is not, chance.'

This could, I think, be seen as corresponding to Hamlet's consciousness of the element of chance at the end of the play, though unlike Mallarmé's, Hamlet's expression of it is specifically Christian. In his speech which begins 'Not a whit, we defy augury . . . ' (v. ii.220), Hamlet both accepts the agency of chance in the *moment* of death ('If it be now, 'tis not to come . . . ' etc.), and yet believes that *sub specie aeternitatis* the event is not random ('There is a special providence in the fall of a sparrow').

V. *Il Se Couche au Tombeau.* 'On the ashes of the stars, those undivided ashes of the family, lay the poor personage, having drunk the drop of the void absent from the sea. (The empty phial, madness, all that remains of the castle?) The Void departed, the castle of purity remains.'

It will appear from this attempt at a resumé that *Igitur* is not an easy work! My part-translation part-description can only be marginally adequate to give a sense of the piece. But there do seem to be tantalizing and suggestive glimpses of meaning to be found in it. It seems to be about a kind of purification of the self, a separation of the self from tradition and the inherited wisdom of the race in order to continue the life of the race; and about the admission of chance into action in order finally to deny chance. There are features which recall *Hamlet*, transposed from the plane of actuality to that of symbol, of a symbolic drama of changing states of soul. There is a ghost, the 'frottement familier et continu d'un âge supérieur', who seems to preside over Igitur in the early stages but not the later ones. There seems to be something proud and possessive in this personified 'race' which wants to gather up its ashes and see itself personified in a new self. The continuation of tradition here seems too personal, too much a matter of ego. The brooding presence comes to be felt as a weight which is essentially part of the temporal ('la sensation de fini'), which has to be crystallized out into that temporal world of clock, furniture, and book, which in the end Igitur separates from himself and which congeals forever as a part of the finitude of death and nothingness which is distinguished from the 'Infinite' of the spirit.

The process here seems to be similar to that in Mallarmé's 'Tombeaux' poems, where the tombs themselves come to represent the solidity and pride of the temporal, the black void of meaningless life which is all that is left of the dead poets whom these poems celebrate. It is only in the structure of the language of the poems that the breath of life can be caught and sustained. Gautier's tomb in 'Toast Funèbre' is

> Le sépulcre solide où gît tout ce qui nuit,
> Et l'avare silence et la massive nuit.[13]

This is the final reality. But in the poem the poet creates a vital illusion:

> Moi, de votre désir soucieux, je veux voir,
> À qui s'évanouit, hier, dans le devoir
> Idéal que nous font les jardins de cet astre,
> Survivre pour l'honneur du tranquille désastre
> Une agitation solennelle par l'air
> De paroles, pourpre ivre et grand calice clair,
> Que, pluie et diamant, le regard diaphane
> Resté là sur ces fleurs dont nulle ne se fane,
> Isole parmi l'heure et le rayon du jour![14]   (p. 55)

Igitur similarly has to separate his action and creation from the mass of materiality symbolized by clock, furniture etc. What this 'creation' is in his case is difficult to suggest precisely, but it could be described as the creation of his Self. The 'drama' treats in terms of states of soul and perceptions of the self what the later 'Tombeaux' poems treat in terms of art and the writing of poetry. And we may feel that the latter are more successful works of art because the creation that is being evoked is there before us, with its own independent life. *Igitur* remains rather more a kind of private exorcism of the uncreative, the act whereby Mallarmé frees himself in order to create.

Having prepared himself Igitur finally acts by throwing the dice. This action admits chance in order to deny it. One can perhaps explain this by saying that if we 'deny chance' in the sense of denying it scope, not allowing for its part in life, we thereby confirm its existence because we confirm our fear of it. But if we act in such a way as to allow for the possibility of chance we effectively deny our belief in its power. We give chance a chance in order to demonstate our faith in its ineffectuality. The act of throwing the dice Mallarmé therefore calls 'folie utile' – useful madness: madness because it abandons reason, decision, calculation; useful because it in effect denies our belief in chance, randomness, and affirms our belief in an ultimate necessity and order. To quote the 'scheme' of Act IV of *Igitur*: 'Brief in an act where chance is in play, it is always chance which accomplishes its proper Idea in confirming or denying itself. Before its existence denial and affirmation both fail. It contains the Absurd – implies it, but in a latent state, and prevents it from existing: which allows the Infinite to be.'

Again we may recall *Hamlet*. Hamlet does not act decisively at the end of the play, I suggest, but gives himself up to chance. Critics have called it Providence, but Bradley seems right when he says it is more like fatalism, a belief in Providence involving the determination to carry out what seems to be the will of Providence. Mallarmé's *Igitur* suggests the possibility of giving oneself up to chance without thereby demonstrating a mere weary fatalism.

Another idea which one can glimpse in *Igitur*, and which associates the piece with certain themes in *Hamlet*, is that of the difference between a real and a false self. Igitur speaks of the 'duality' of his *personnage*, and of his 'dernière figure' (final appearance or face) separated from his *personnage* by *une fraise arachnéenne* (an arachnian or finely spun ruff or collar). He also speaks of 'stripping off, through thought, the disguise (*travestissement*) imposed on me by the necessity of living in the heart of this race, the sole remaining source of ambiguity', and of 'disengaging my dream from this costume'. In a margin-note to section IV

22

entitled 'Scène de Théatre, Ancien Igitur', he refers to himself as 'comédien' – comedian or actor. The 'fraise' or 'ruff' has distinct Elizabethan overtones, but more important is the general association with the idea of Hamlet's 'antic disposition'; his awareness of *his* costume (his 'inky cloak' and 'customary suits of solemn black') and of the possibilities of over-acted grief ('actions that a man might play') in i.ii; his advice to the Players on the dangers of literally over-acting; his fleeting imagination of himself getting 'a fellowship in a cry of players' (iii.ii. 284); and his over-violent and theatrical self-castigation in his soliloquy after hearing the First Player's Priam speech (ii.ii. 559–617). He tests the King's conscience by putting on a play, and in the end meets his death by his agreement to 'play' (v.ii. 254 and in the stage directions) at fencing with Laertes, just as Igitur has to 'jouer le tour' (play the turn) at dice. Both are aware of the problems of real action as against 'playing'. In Igitur's case he is aware of the pathos and theatricality of himself as a *personnage* or 'character', but nevertheless 'with the help of' this character the Act can be carried out and chance denied.

Mallarmé seems then to be writing a kind of *Hamlet* of the mind, inspired by the play but rendering its problems in a totally new form. He has himself broken away from tradition and rendered the myth afresh. We can hardly say that *Igitur* is a successful work of art: it is probably too obscure, not fully realized. Much of it is naked metaphysic, and the symbolic furniture does not always seem to have enough necessary connection with the subject. The same symbols often reappear in the later poetry, but there they are more fully charged with significance and detached from the leading strings of the metaphysic. But still the metaphysic, expressed partly in abstractions, partly in symbols, seems to have been necessary for Mallarmé. As he said in a letter to Cazalis in 1869:

It is a tale, by which I wish to throw off the old monster of Impotence, – its subject, too – in order to cloister myself in my great labour which I have already taken up again. If it is done, I am cured.[15]

Igitur finally lies down on the ashes of his ancestors. It is a kind of artistic self-destruction to allow the rebirth of the artistic genius. It might be compared in this to Kafka's story 'The Judgement', where the protagonist is condemned to death by his father and leaps to his death from a bridge. The last sentence reads: 'At that moment an endless stream of traffic was passing over the bridge.' The writer symbolically kills himself, but his perception of life just detaches itself and survives. After writing the story Kafka spoke of it in terms similar to Mallarmé's comment in the letter. He wrote it in a single night, and felt 'as if I were advancing over water. Several times during the night I heaved my own weight on my back.'

Could the same kind of effort be seen in Shakespeare's *Hamlet*? The play marks a turning-point in his art, from what had previously consisted of romantic comedy and historical drama to the profound and full creativity, the comprehensiveness of the great tragedies. Hamlet is the first of the great tragic heroes, and differs from the others, as I shall argue below, in the ambiguity of his guilt and innocence, and in the way he spends the whole play hesitating before action, before actually, one might say, *becoming* tragic (if he really does). Can we see Shakespeare himself here, hovering in front of the conception of the tragic before finally immersing himself in it, before sinking himself in a conception of life which necessarily involves the destruction of the good and the great – their self-destruction, but a destruction in which we see that goodness and greatness most fully manifested? *Troilus and Cressida* seems to be a kind of nadir in Shakespeare's vision, presenting all in a spirit of doubt and confusion, almost cynicism, where all love and heroism are hypocritical, and all greatness is doubtful in its very foundations. In the tragedies the heroes are profoundly wrong in their actions but their greatness is manifested nevertheless. In *Hamlet* the hero is caught between these two worlds. The vision is much of the time that of *Troilus and Cressida* but it seems to be waiting, like the hero of that play, for something else.[16] And in the end the hero goes, in whatever spirit, to meet his destiny and death. He, and the play, commit themselves to tragedy.

Igitur suggests a possible symbolic substructure for *Hamlet*. Hamlet has to act, to carry out what appears to be a duty enjoined on him by his father's ghost, just as Igitur's duty is enjoined on him by his ancestors. Hamlet hesitates but does not know why. He suffers a radical impotence of will. He seems towards the end of the play to be less concerned with the memory of the ghost, just as Igitur moves away from the presence of the spirit of his ancestors. He gives

24

himself up to chance – with gestures towards 'a divinity that shapes our ends' – but mainly to chance. He is weighed down in the course of the play by the paraphernalia of time – Polonius's busybodying, Rosencrantz and Guildenstern's time-serving, Ophelia's frailty, the fatuity of Osric. From these he has to detach himself and cast the dice. 'Rashly, and praised by rashness for it. . . ' 'If it be now, 'tis not to come. If it be not now, yet it will come.' 'I shall win at the odds.' And at the end of the play, Horatio speaks of 'accidental judgements, causal slaughters'. Certainly, these events of the play, because they are drawn on a plane of actuality, involve other problems, most notably moral ones. We may praise rashness in theory – but the killing of Polonius? Mallarmé's drama is played out on a meta-physical plane and so avoids such problems. But it is possible to see this drama lying potentially within Shakespeare's, and to suggest that Shakespeare's play can be seen to be exploring the fundamental questions of action: how to act so as to transcend the contingent while allowing the inevitability of chance; how to act from a deep centre, 'the intuition of the soul', so as to destroy the ego, realize the true Self, and continue the life of the race.

Mallarmé's essay on *Hamlet* of 1886 will perhaps clarify some of these ideas.[17] He is writing about the performance of Mounet-Sully at the Comédie Française. He sees the play, as one might expect, as the 'solitary drama' of Hamlet, and its subject as 'the antagonism of the dream in man to the fatalities layed on his existence by unhappiness'. He complains that Laertes is too prominent in the classical heroic vein, whereas everything in the play should be subordinate to Hamlet himself and indeed simply a lesser expression of his dilemma. ('He who revolves around an exceptional character like Hamlet is only another Hamlet').

So Mallarmé concentrates almost entirely on Hamlet's character. He speaks of 'the morbid dualism which constitutes Hamlet's case'. But behind this lies 'the latent man of nobility whom he cannot become', and this is the supreme spectacle which the stage exists to defend. The perception of dualism is the essential thing. For Hamlet cannot be *either* the 'sweet prince' *or* the 'arrant knave': he must be both; but his nobility remains only latent, 'a jewel intact beneath the disaster'. On the surface there is disaster and evil.

Mounet-Sully created the Hamlet of his time, in France, by summing up 'the fine demon', 'after the anguished Romantic eve'. That is, it would seem that, for Mallarmé, Mounet-Sully's Hamlet is significant in its crystallization of the evil in the hero after the ambiguities of the Romantic reading.

In his additional note on the play, 'Hamlet and Fortinbras', written in 1896, Mallarmé intensifies this sense of the play, when he speaks of Hamlet's egoism 'denying others with a look'. 'He kills indifferently, or rather, people die. The black presence of the doubter causes this poison, so that all the great ones die: without his always taking the trouble to kill them behind the arras.' By 1896, therefore, Mallarmé has come to place even more emphasis on the 'demon' in Hamlet. In the same piece he talks of 'the sumptuous and stagnant exaggeration of murder around one who makes himself solitary', and of how this 'stagnant pond' is voided by the vulgar arrival of Fortinbras, 'within the vulgar comprehension of every-body, amid the drums and the trumpets'. There seems to be an ambivalent feeling here that Hamlet is decadent and poisonous but that, in comparison with his exceptional nature, the ordinary heroism of someone like Fortinbras is tawdry and vulgar. Some such feeling may associate itself with the change of artistic feeling which caused Mallarmé to write another version, as one may call it, of *Igitur*, in his last poem, 'Un Coup de Dés'.

This extraordinary poem, impossible to quote from accurately because of its typography, evokes not the calm of age but the staggerings of a mind caught in the shipwreck of life. There is a sense of desperation, but of desperation controlled and formulated into an exact symbol. It is a reconsideration of the domination of chance over life, and has a renewed sense of the impossibility of man's controlling his fate. Chance can no longer be 'absorbed' as in *Igitur*: the throw of the dice cannot abolish chance. And instead of bringing about a final action and a reconciliation between man and his fate and between man and his race – where, as in *Igitur*, man can finally blow out the candle in peace and compose himself on the ashes of his ancestors – we have here a maelstrom of action, the dice thrown in the height of the storm. The hero, whom we just glimpse in the poem, is forgotten at the end, and we are left simply with the number formed by the dice, which *may* become something permanent, a constellation. The whole poem is a symbol of Mallarmé's art: it is about the act of creation. It bears little on the fate of the poet who has to submit to the storm, but the throw of the dice is like the throw of words on the page. They are thrown there, and once thrown they form a pattern, like a constellation of stars. The central statement of the poem, in large capital letters, 'UN COUP DE DÉS JAMAIS N'ABOLIRA LE HASARD', is surrounded by a whirl of subordinate clauses which cannot negate the statement but seems to lift it out of its condition as mere statement, and place it typographically, and for the ear, among a cluster of lesser words. The negative statement takes its place as part of a pattern, a constellation of words; in which condition it moves forever, permanent and unchangeable, not subject to chance. Mallarmé once wrote: 'Chance can never invade a line of verse', and here verse becomes the element in which language can rise above its function as 'meaning' or 'signification' and achieve a timeless pattern. The meaning of the central statement cannot be denied, but the poem lifts the words above this meaning, as it were, and lets them ride in a freer atmosphere, above time and change.

The 'hero' of this poem, if we can call him that, therefore takes a subordinate place. We can call him both Igitur and Igitur's successor, or a young Hamlet, the 'bitter prince of reefs', 'a dainty dark form standing upright', the boyish shadow of the Old Master mentioned at the beginning of the poem. As in *Hamlet* there is an old hero who bequeaths a duty to a younger figure, and as in the play the older figure is suffering the buffetings of fate, the shipwreck of existence, as much as the younger. The younger figure becomes identified by the feather in his cap (perhaps the other meaning of 'plume' – a pen – may be recalled).

```
plume solitaire éperdue
    sauf    que la rencontre ou l'effleure une toque de minuit
                        et immobilise
            au velours chiffonné par un esclaffement sombre
                    cette blancheur rigide
            dérisoire
                        en opposition au ciel
            trop
                    pour ne pas marquer
                    exigüment
                        quiconque
            prince amer de l'écueil
```

27

s'en coiffe comme de l'héroïque
irrésistible mais contenu
par sa petite raison virile
en foudre

soucieux

    expiatoire et pubère[18]   (pp. 468–71)

And later this feather falls, to be lost in the waves:

Choit
  la plume
    rythmique suspense du sinistre
         s'ensevelir
         aux écumes originelles[19] (p. 473)

This fall has 'no human result'. The action in itself is empty and the waves lap over it to obliterate it, in case (by claiming significance) 'by its lie it might have founded perdition in these regions of the wave where all reality dissolves'. (We may think of the damnation founded by the heroism of Milton's Satan.) There is no praise of heroic action in this poem. The point of the action lies not in the heroism but simply in the action itself.

As a development of the myth of the young prince this does perhaps show some connection with Mallarmé's writing on *Hamlet* in 1896, the year before this poem was written. There Hamlet's self-absorption, the poison of his doubt, is emphasized. He causes a sumptuous and stagnant exaggeration of murder. He cannot be seen as a hero. And yet by him the act – the purification of his race – is carried out. He cannot act with decision and conscious aim but submits himself to chance. In what spirit does he finally kill the King: in a spirit of weary fatalism, of justice, of murderous revenge? It is a question about which critics have reached no satisfactory conclusions. Mallarmé's short piece of 1896 suggests that he sees Hamlet more and more as a negative and destructive figure. But supposing one shared the view, would we then wish that Hamlet had *not* killed the King? Or, to put it aesthetically rather than morally, could the logic of the play have been different? By Claudius's death Denmark is purged of a murderous king; the race has been purified. It is possible to say that the action is right, or aesthetically fitting, without thereby saying that Hamlet has been heroic and moral. If Hamlet submits to chance this cannot be a

28

moral action. As a statement of belief it implies nihilism, despair, moral defeat. Yet because of it the pattern of the action is completed. The play, the total constellation of words and actions, exists over and above the moral statement or lack of statement which Hamlet's action embodies.

Hamlet's action cannot 'abolish chance' but neither does it affirm it. Hamlet does not reach a resolved state of mind (I suggest), but nor does he act irresponsibly. He simply acts, in response to pressures from outside. His action shows no 'commitment', but neither does it demonstrate lack of commitment. It is simply action, which completes the pattern and ends the play. Hamlet throws the dice, and by so doing projects the constellation of all his actions into the firmament. The play is Shakespeare's central meditation on the problem of action. He cannot bring Hamlet to the point of *decisive* action, cannot entirely free him from the stagnant pool of impotence. Yet the action is accomplished. Events move to the end. Hamlet acts, non-morally, and completes the action of the whole. As an artist, Shakespeare throws the dice and projects the play into its timeless state. No 'statement' can be derived from the play – or rather, since the play cannot avoid the level of statement entirely, the statement contained in it is caught up and made to serve something beyond itself. As a statement the play says that man can never know himself and therefore cannot act with decision. Hamlet's death is not triumphant. Even Horatio is baffled. We are left with a host of unanswered questions. The 'character' of Hamlet is an unsolvable riddle. But the heroic 'character' is, as in *Igitur*, something of an anachronism; the 'character', or *personnage* of Igitur, is something which helps the hero towards his end, but is finally discarded – one might call it the ego, the personality. But beyond the problem of the 'character', the action is completed and the race is purified. Perhaps no action or thought can be genuinely decisive, made in the firm knowledge of motives and ends. But nevertheless action can create life and throw into constellation something permanent. 'Every thought emits a dice throw', wrote Mallarmé in the last line of 'Un Coup de Dés': a dice throw which contains an inevitable element of contingency, but which, thrown, comes to rest as a final constellation. Bounded in a nutshell by his temporal condition, the artist can still become king of infinite space.

29

2

'What may this mean?'
Claudel and Valéry

'Il se promène. . . lisant au livre de lui-même' – so Mallarmé, in perhaps the most striking of his formulations about Hamlet (in 'Hamlet and Fortinbras'). For this is indeed what Hamlet does throughout the play. When Polonius finds him reading, the book may be by. . .whom? Montaigne? but the thoughts he pretends to find in it are his own. He studies and questions himself throughout the play as he has been accustomed to study the world. He imputes to himself a hidden meaning – 'I have that within that passes show'; he writes down his thoughts – 'Meet it is I set it down'; he questions his nature – 'What should such fellows as I do?', what the world means to him – 'What is this quintessence of dust?', and what constitutes life and death, whether he should live or die, what life he should lead – 'To be or not to be, that is the question.' He is a book whose meaning he can never fathom, full of indecipherable signs. Before he dies he begs Horatio to decipher him to the world:

O God, Horatio, what a wounded name,
Things standing thus unknown, shall live behind me!   (v.ii. 345–6)

Not only Hamlet but the whole play is like an indecipherable sign, full of events the participants do not understand.

— Who's there?
— Nay, answer me. Stand and unfold yourself.   (I.i. 1–2)

The opening words might almost be the play's epigraph. Hamlet challenges the Universe but has to unfold himself. The Ghost is the greatest of the mysteries, 'thing', 'shape', 'it'. 'What art thou?' is Horatio's first speech to it. As things progress the ghost leaves more and more signs to decipher. When it fades on the crowing of the

30

cock it is for Marcellus an intelligible sign suggesting an evil spirit. The activities of the Danish army are enigmatic signs for Marcellus. Hamlet in the first court scene is another mystery for the rest of the court. 'Why seems it [his father's death] so particular with thee?', asks the King. And Hamlet points to an inner meaning, a grief which he reveals and hides at once.

Hamlet is an unknown quantity for Laertes and Polonius. His actions towards them are signs of doubtful import, but they suspect the worst. Laertes tries out his own interpretation on Ophelia; so does Polonius, who also solicits more evidence – 'What is't between you?' Ophelia speaks of 'tenders of his affection': these too are signs, but Polonius reads them a different way, as 'springes to catch woodcocks'. Later, in sending Reynaldo after Laertes, Polonius again boasts himself a connoisseur of signs, and tells Reynaldo how to discover and read them,

> With windlasses and with assays of bias,
> By indirections find directions out.   (II.i. 65–6)

Hamlet in his 'distemper' becomes an enigmatic sign for the King and Queen. They too ask in effect, 'What does this mean?' – 'What it should be', says the King, 'I cannot dream of'. For Rosencrantz and Guildenstern Hamlet's utterances are riddles:

> — Prison, my lord?
> — Denmark's a prison.   (II.ii. 246–7)

Later Hamlet accuses them of trying to play on him like a pipe – 'you would seem to know my stops; you would pluck out the heart of my mystery'.

The most enigmatic sign, for Hamlet himself, is of course the Ghost. He puts on the play to try to reveal the significance of this sign. Whether it does fully reveal that significance I leave for the moment an open question. Hamlet seems to think it does. The King's behaviour is a sign which Hamlet urges Horatio to watch closely: 'Even with the very comment of thy soul observe my uncle', but, as has been recently suggested,[1] the sign may not be as unambiguous as Hamlet thinks it, and Horatio seems to give it guarded credence. And after this the play's enigmas are still not exhausted. Hamlet interprets his escape from the pirates and his chance to change the message to England as heavenly signs – 'Why even in this was heaven ordinant', and 'There's a divinity that shapes our ends.' But it is not clear that we should accept them thus so readily and see heaven to be as unconcerned with the deaths of Rosencrantz and Guildenstern as Hamlet is. Osric talks in high-falutin riddles which, as Horatio says, need notes in the margin. Even when Hamlet understands his message, the meaning of the duel – why it has been set up – remains obscure to him. But at this point Hamlet gives up the attempt to read the signs – 'We defy augury.'

At the end of the play the signs are still unread by the survivors. Horatio is commissioned to decipher them. But to Fortinbras's question, 'Where is this sight?', Horatio replies, 'What is it you would see?'

> If aught of woe or wonder, cease your search.   (v.ii. 364)

Fortinbras questions, the English Ambassador questions. Horatio promises to deliver an account of 'accidental judgements, casual slaughters', 'purposes mistook', 'carnal, bloody, and unnatural acts' – but he says nothing of the *interpretation* of them. Fortinbras ends the play by ordering for Hamlet 'the soldiers' music and the rite of war', a final symbolization of Hamlet's heroism as Fortinbras conceives it. The first time we heard cannons go off in the play was in i.iv, when Horatio's talk of the Ghost was interrupted with the sound of Claudius's festivities and Horatio asked, 'What does this mean?' Now, the last sound in the play, a peal of ordnance is shot off. Does it finally establish the play's recognition of Hamlet's heroism or does it not rather reverberate with unanswered questions? What does this mean?

This brief account of the play as an enigmatic sign, full of signs, takes its beginning from Mallarmé's sentence, and also from an essay of Paul Claudel, 'Le Catastrophe d'Igitur'.

Supreme Hamlet, at the top of his tower...while the inexorable night around him makes him forever *un homme d'intérieur*, sees that he is surrounded by objects whose function is to *signify*, that he is enclosed in a prison of signs.[2]

This makes of him, writes Claudel, 'un professeur d'attention' – a teacher of attentiveness, or perhaps of 'waiting'. Mallarmé, Claudel goes on, is the prince of the modern Elsinore. He is the first to place himself before reality not as a spectacle but as a *text*, confronting it with the question, 'What does it mean?' Claudel's essay is the culmination of the tendency to equate Hamlet and the modern spirit. Hamlet becomes Mallarmé, and the play a symbolist poem. But as I've tried to suggest by following through the implications of this in relation to the play, the parallel is not just of historical interest in relation to the Symbolists. It gives us a way of seeing the play which is still suggestive – which sees it as *about* the problem of interpretation.

There is a postscript to add. An essay by Paul Valéry published in *The Athenæum* in 1919 uses *Hamlet* as an image for a slightly different idea, and one which points forward to T. S. Eliot. In 'La Crise de l'Esprit',[3] Valéry sees the modern intellect as typified by its heterogeneity, its mixture of fragments of past culture. This notion – here it seems merely that – will remind readers of the idea that Eliot 'created' fully in *The Waste Land*. There we feel and see the nature of such a mind. In the present connection it is notable that Valéry draws on *Hamlet* to describe the condition.

The European Hamlet watches a million Ghosts... He has for his phantoms all the objects of our controversies.

This passing use of the Ghost in *Hamlet* as an image for the phantoms of tradition seems significant. It recalls Mallarmé's preoccupation with the ancestral ghosts of Igitur; and it points forward to Eliot's profound use of the ghost in 'Little Gidding' as an embodiment of traditional wisdom, his 'dead masters'. *Hamlet* incorporates itself in the imagination of Mallarmé, Valéry and Eliot as an image of the relation between tradition and creation. The prison of signs in which Hamlet is locked is not of his own making merely. In seeking to unlock it he must define his relation to the past, his duty towards it, and his need for freedom from it.

3

'Your only jig-maker'
Jules Laforgue

Laforgue made a pilgrimage to Elsinore on New Year's Day, 1886. The gesture typifies the whimsical, nostalgic relation of the French poet to Shakespeare's play and, in particular, to its hero. From the character of Hamlet Laforgue fashioned the mask of the failed hero through which sounded the delicate self-mocking ariettes of his verse. Quotations from *Hamlet* provide the epigraphs for several of his poems in *Des Fleurs de Bonne Volonté* (the collection of poetic fragments made after his death), and these poems are often the early sketches for the longer poems in *Derniers Vers*, which is usually regarded as his most successful volume. Perhaps the best known of his *Moralités Légendaires* – the collection of ironically retold myths – is 'Hamlet; ou les Suites de la Piété Filiale'.

Laforgue made of Hamlet an ironic decadent of the late nineteenth century. But in so doing he created a figure who could stand for the poet himself: a means by which he could test his aspirations and separate genuine perceptions from egoism and self-consciousness. By wearing the mask of Hamlet, Laforgue managed to shed some of the crudity, and even cruelty, of his earlier verse, becoming more aware of it and gradually excluding it or qualifying it by irony and self-criticism. He mocked his own callowness by exploring Hamlet's: he eased the burden of an uneasy sexuality by contemplating and parodying the intense mockery and disgust that Hamlet expresses.

The crudity of some of his early verse can be represented by a few lines from 'Guitare'. Laforgue lists interminably and with schoolboyish glee the horrors which await his beloved in the grave:

> Tout pourrira! Vos mains qui [re]tenaient les guides
> Au bois de si noble façon,

Jules Laforgue

Votre ventre, peau flasque et se creusant de rides
    Votre cervelle de pinson,
Vos intestins sucrés, vos pieds souples d'almée,
    Vos poumons roses, votre cœur,
Et votre clitoris qui vous tordrait pâmée
    En de longs spasmes de langueur.[1]

It was from this kind of thing that his concern with Hamlet helped him to escape, for Hamlet shares this morbid fascination but is more self-critical of it and more serious about it. Laforgue's earlier poems tend to be straightforwardly personal and hence sometimes embarrassing and open to the charge of self-pity. The gloom is often heavily laid on, as in 'Litanies de misère', which 'traces the history of the world to the birth of man',[2] and concludes with stanzas describing life after man's coming:

La femme hurle aux nuits, se tord et mord les draps
Pour pondre des enfants vils, malheureux, ingrats.

La moitié meurt avant un an, dans la misère,
Sans compter les morts-nés bons à cacher sous terre.

L'homme, les fleurs, les nids, tout sans trêve travaille,
Car la vie à chaque heure est une âpre bataille.[3]   (pp. 325–6)

In the first substantial volume, *Les Complaintes* of 1885, this melodramatic solemnity is often mitigated by irony, as in the poem 'Complainte du Pauvre Chevalier-Errant'. But nevertheless the charm of this poem is in its lightly comic pathos; it contains little serious self-criticism. Its tone is summed up by the way the Knight-Errant of the title becomes by the end the poor sandwich-man parading his sign:

Au Bon Chevalier-Errant,
Restaurant,
Hôtel meublé, Cabinets de lecture, prix courants.[4]   (p. 74)

'Petites Misères', the disarming title of a number of these poems, also sums up the mixture of complaint, sadness, foolery and self-mockery. Their main quality is their whimsical charm. It is not until *Derniers Vers* that there is any dynamic dramatic quality to these meditations, a quality like that of Eliot's 'Portrait of a Lady' where we feel that there is a conflict within the poem, that the poet

35

is using his irony not as a means simply of self-display, but of self-analysis and serious clarification. For there is a danger in self-mockery of trivialization: it is possible for a comic poet not to take himself seriously enough.

Michael Collie has suggested, and it seems convincing, that Laforgue achieved a greater detachment from his own lightly mocked 'misères' partly through his experiments with myth in the *Moralités Légendaires*.[5] Of these the 'Hamlet' is the first, and in itself shows a gain in self-awareness. It is a parody of *Hamlet* and it is also a parody of the nineteenth-century dilettante, Laforgue himself. In a setting heavy with *bibelots* and *objets d'art*, the pale hero delicately and languidly drags his small feminine feet around his chamber, smokes Turkish and English cigarettes and dreams of being a Parisian playwright. But the story may be briefly summarized.[6]

Hamlet lives in a wing of the castle at Elsinore, above a stagnant pond, and next to a refuse heap on which are thrown the bouquets and other detritus of royal festivities. His window looks out across the Sound towards Norway, where Fortinbras, active and energetic, leads the life of the true leader. On the walls of Hamlet's chamber hang a portrait of himself (his smile surrounded by a 'sulphurous penumbra'); a dozen views of Jutland, on one of which he spits in heroic disgust; and a portrait of his father. Other decorations are two wax statuettes of his mother and step-father, Gerutha and Fengo, with pins stuck into them *puérilement*; and in an alcove – *hélas* – a shower apparatus. The landscape in the story is enlivened with touches of pathetic Pathetic Fallacy: the waves of the Sound play animatedly with the sailors – 'but it is the only feeling allowed them'. Hamlet is treated as a consciously (and self-consciously) literary figure ('Who has not heard of his *yeux d'hirondelle de mer?*'), and the period is self-consciously 'period' ('the stuff of a fine seventeenth-century soirée').

This Hamlet (like Shakespeare's) keeps notebooks to help stimulate vengeance for his father, 'irregularly deceased'. But they have merely developed his taste for writing ('Je pris goût à l'œuvre'). Hamlet recites his poems (Laforgue's own), suffers *petites misères* such as the difficulty of tearing up Ophelia's letters, and murmurs 'It's all heredity'. He soliloquizes heroically, 'To Act! To kill!'; he dreams of liberty, of writing, of marriage. On his way through the corridors of the palace he seizes a canary from a cage, wrings its neck, and throws it in the lap of a nearby waiting-woman, who looks up enraptured to declare she has always loved him. 'Another one!', he mutters. He excuses his violence to himself by saying that he is merely trying out his hand for vengeance. He goes hunting in the forest, killing its creatures with maniacal abandon, putting out their eyes and cracking their bones.

He pays a visit to the graveyard. On the way there he muses about social reform, dreaming of a 'fraternal childhood on Earth' – an earthly Paradise. He treads on an anthill 'so that Chance should be in his debt'. At the graveyard he learns that Yorick the clown was in fact his brother, and that their mother died at Hamlet's birth. The gravedigger praises Laertes for his sympathetic interest in the Artisans' Dwelling question. Hamlet meditates on the insignificance of the world and on his own genius. He is a Messiah, but a spoiled Messiah. 'How superiorly bored I am!', he drawls. Witnessing Ophelia's funeral he consoles himself that she would only have grown up to become Fortinbras's mistress and to die of shame.

He returns to overlook the preparation of his play, to be performed that evening before the King and Queen, which he has given to the actors Kate and William to prepare. He finds Kate weeping: she has been so moved by his play that she has decided to enter a religious order. But Hamlet, who has fallen in love with her, persuades her to elope with him after the play. The play is a success: the King leaves in anger. Hamlet decides that the King has been punished enough, and he and Kate ride off into the night, towards a life of writing and acting in Paris. The night is calm. 'The moon performs, not without success, the enchantment of polar nights.' Hamlet stops to pick a flower from his father's tomb. There he encounters Laertes: they fight, and Hamlet is killed. He dies, gasping '*Qualis...artifex... pereo*', and 'renders up to the Infinite his Hamletic soul'. Kate returns to William to be beaten for her folly and the story concludes: 'One Hamlet more or less; the race isn't lost because of that, one says to oneself.'

This whimsical *fin-de-siècle* version of Hamlet's story is no doubt typical of its time and typical of Laforgue. Its elegant absurdity and parody are meant mainly to amuse. But like all good parodies, it is close enough to the original to contain some pertinent criticism.

Hamlet's melancholy, his impulsive violence and brutality, the feeling that he was born to reform society, the metaphysical musings, the self-mockery, the good looks, the tortured but indecisive concern with his father's death, even the enthusiasm for the theatre, are all twisted just out of key into the discordant music of farce.

And in mocking Hamlet Laforgue is criticizing himself. The details of the mad hunting scene are violent enough to be genuinely disturbing, and to make us think again about Hamlet's killing of Polonius or his sparing of Claudius in order to send him to hell. It also makes us think again about the sadistic element in an early poem of Laforgue's such as 'Guitare', or of the taunting morbidity beneath the humour of 'Excuse Macabre', where the poet holds up his beloved's skull and says 'I can certainly sell it, can't I Margaretha?' He is mocking himself too in the passages where Hamlet dreams of a Messianic role, or of the pettiness of earth 'ticketed with a pitiful *idem* in the list of evolution' (which echoes one of his poems).

In so far as we can speak of development in relation to such a short poetic career, the development of Laforgue's poetry springs from the conflict between taking himself too seriously and not taking himself seriously enough. We see the former fault in the earliest poems, then the latter. In the *Dernier Vers* we can say that he has struck a balance between the two. And reading *Hamlet*, writing his parody, and adopting Hamlet's tone contributed to this process.

The visit to Elsinore on 1 January 1886 was commemorated in a little piece Laforgue wrote for the magazine *Le Symboliste*,[7] and is worth examining for what it reveals of Laforgue's preoccupations with *Hamlet*. Laforgue imagines himself interviewing the prince, who asks what has become of his legend. Laforgue replies that Irving's interpretation, which he saw in Berlin, was too solemn, 'se prenant trop au sérieux' – 'which certainly', Laforgue adds, 'was never the case with a distinguished man like you, eh?' And in Paris? Paul Bourget cultivates the legend, Rimbaud dies of it, and Laforgue himself keeps alive the spirit of Yorick. 'And what have they made of Ophelia?', Hamlet asks. 'Ah – it's what she's made of us', replies Laforgue. No longer a pious believer, she has turned religion into a marriage bait; but she is more irresistible than ever; and Laforgue quotes his poem 'La Femme, mûre ou jeune fille'. At the end of it

Hamlet cries out, 'Aux armes, citoyens, il n'y a plus de raison.' And his contagious madness causes Laforgue to do a little dance symbolizing the square of the hypotenuse – 'the paradigm of human certitude' – a dance which always makes the dancer fall over. 'Now this dance being symbolic of the First Mover . . .' – and here the piece ends.

The article appeared just before the publication of Laforgue's 'Hamlet'. It shows his whimsical view of the hero, and himself, and his light mockery of human certainties. It also suggests the importance of Ophelia in his reaction to the play. For the question of love and marriage is one of the recurring refrains of Laforgue's melancholy humour. He is entangled in exquisite threads which draw him in opposite directions: he wants his young ladies to preserve their virginal purity ('To a nunnery, go'), and at the same time to provide him with solace. He longs for a wife, and yet his delicate soul recoils in aesthetic horror from the banalities of family life. Out of the confusions of what he calls his 'pauvre âme adolescente' come the pathetic and wistful little songs, lifted all the time out of mawkishness by their light melodies, their studiedly careless gestures, and their veiled astringencies. Is the fault in him, or in women themselves? *Could* he make a husband? What of the physical facts? What of his art – would she understand him? Meanwhile the wind blusters outside, and the showers sweep against the window-panes. *Ah! Petites misères d' automne!*

The *Derniers Vers* show the humorous toying with these things at its most poetical. They also show a more developed range of feeling. And Laforgue's reading of *Hamlet* seems to be involved in the development. In the edited fragments of *Des Fleurs de Bonne Volonté* are several poems with epigraphs from the play, mainly from the Ophelia scenes. In poem XVI, entitled 'Dimanches' like many of Laforgue's poems (his could be called the poetry of wet Sunday afternoons), the epigraph is from Hamlet's 'Have you a daughter? . . . Let her not walk i' the sun; conception is a blessing; but not as your daughter may conceive'. The poem is a light piece of humorous pathos. It is raining; the poet is looking out of the window; a group of schoolgirls is passing, many – 'ô pauvres chairs!' – without overcoats. One of them suddenly breaks away from the others and runs away. She throws herself into the river. No one about, nothing to be done!

Le crépuscule vient; le petit port
Allume ses feux. (Ah! connu, l'décor!).

La pluie continue à mouiller le fleuve,
Le ciel pleut sans but, sans que rien l'émeuve.[8]   (p. 215)

Laforgue's subject is the Ophelia of the suburbs. The epigraph is only loosely connected with the poem (does it, perhaps, give a hint of why the young girl drowns herself?), but it is used to typify a mood of weary fatalism. Shakespeare's Hamlet is doubtless harsher than Laforgue's speaker, but Laforgue selects what he needs. The poet looks on helplessly: he is not the heroic saviour. (And here, is Shakespeare's Hamlet so very different?)

Poem XXVIII, another 'Dimanches', is interesting because in *Derniers Vers* it is developed into a fuller poem which shows a shift of sensibility. The epigraph is the bawdy dialogue from the play scene 'Lady, shall I lie in your lap?' etc. In tune with the epigraph the tone of this poem is harsher. There is a mood of comic frustration and rage:

Les nasillardes cloches des dimanches
A l'étranger,
Me font que j'ai de la vache enragée.[9]   (p. 231)

The poet watches the young girl going home. Then the sound of her piano arouses him. He imagines her heart stammering in scurrilous jigs, her flesh – 'sur quoi j'ai de droits' – swooning, and he breaks out into a frenzied

Que je te les tordrais avec plaisir,
Ce cœur, ce corps![10]

Like Hamlet in the epigraph, but more lightly and whimsically, Laforgue gives vent to his sexual feelings in snatches of wit.

In *Derniers Vers*, poem III, the lustful irritation of the early version is toned down. The 'ritournelles si infâmes' of the girl's piano become 'ritournelles de bastringues'. The poem begins not with the irritation of the earlier one but with a minor but significant piece of self-realization:

Bref, j'allais me donner d'un 'Je vous aime'
Quand je m'avisai non sans peine
Que d'abord je ne me possédais pas bien moi-même.[11]   (p. 284)

40

Jules Laforgue

The part from the earlier poem is embedded in a more seriously self-critical context. The sexual relish of 'ce cœur, ce corps' is followed in the later poem by lines which suggest that this mere physicality is not enough; nor is mere spirituality.

> Et ce n'est pas sa chair qui me serait tout,
> Et je ne serais pas qu'un grand cœur pour elle,
> Mais quoi s'en aller faire les fous
> Dans des histoires fraternelles!
> L'âme et la chair, la chair et l'âme,
> C'est l'Esprit édénique et fier
> D'être un peu l'Homme avec la Femme.[12]

The woman cannot be just flesh to him, and he cannot be merely a noble heart to her. Talk of a simply fraternal relationship is also absurd (there is an echo here of Laforgue's Hamlet and his yearning for 'la fraternité d'enfance'). Laforgue is sanely human in this poem, with his feeling for the noble and proud spirit of Eden. The pleasant, shrugging self-awareness is caught charmingly at the end of the poem:

> – Allons, dernier des poètes,
> Toujours enfermé tu te rendras malade!
> Vois, il fait beau temps tout le monde est dehors,
> Va donc acheter deux sous d'ellébore,
> Ça te fera une petite promenade.[13]

The general movement seems to be from a treatment of the subject which draws on the pathos of the young man and the predatoriness of the woman to a more balanced and self-critical view.

In poem XXXIV of *Des Fleurs* the poet says that he will castigate the girl for her seductive arts (like Hamlet to his mother):

> Là, là, je te ferai la honte!
> Et je te demanderai compte
> De ce corset cambrant tes reins,
> De ta tournure et des frisures
> Achalandant contre-nature
> Ton front et ton arrière-train.[14]   (pp. 240–1)

But the poem ends with a weary wish that he could live more in accord with the world's natural goods. In poem XL, 'Petites Misères d'Automne', the girl devours the poet with her eyes, and

41

Ses boudoirs pluvieux mirent en sang
Mon inutile cœur d'adolescent. . .
Et j'en dormis. A l'aube je m'enfuis. . .
Bien égal aujourd'hui.[15]   (p. 252)

The poem has for an epigraph Hamlet's 'Get thee to a nunnery; why wouldst thou be a breeder of sinners? I am myself indifferent honest' etc. Unlike the previous epigraphs, this is the one in which Hamlet begins to turn his criticism against himself. But the tone of the poem is still straightforwardly comically self-pitying. The enlarged version of the poem in *Derniers Vers* has the same epigraph, but is less self-preoccupied. The speaker thinks more about the girl herself. There is in this at once a greater breadth of sympathy, and also a recognition that part of the trouble is that he identifies with her too much – that his pity is also self-pity:

Oh, cette misère de vouloir être notre femme.

He ends up by telling the girl to avoid abandoning herself to the ugly games of married life. He also asks for greater understanding: he invokes Nature to give him strength to love the whole character, 'ce qu'il y a d'histoires' behind her pretty orphan's eyes, and the strength to imagine himself old.

As a final example one might consider poem XLIV of *Des Fleurs de Bonne Volonté* with its epigraph from Laertes's 'The chariest maid is prodigal enough / If she unmask her beauty to the moon.' It is particularly interesting to an English reader because it appears to be Laforgue's version (perhaps a source?) of Eliot's 'Portrait of a Lady'. There is an embarrassed bachelor, who is the speaker, and an effusive lady:

(Des yeux dégustateurs âpres à la curée;
Une bouche à jamais cloîtrée!)

(– Voici qu'elle m'honore de ses confidences;
J'en souffre plus qu'elle ne pense!)[16]   (p. 257)

Half-way through, the verse breaks off into a little melody, a precursor perhaps of the Chopin and the ariettes of cracked cornets in Eliot:

Hier l'orchestre attaqua
Sa dernière polka.[17]

42

Jules Laforgue

At the end of the poem the speaker breaks out against the lady's incessant monologue:

> Va, vos moindres clins d'yeux sont des parjures.
> Tais-toi, avec vous autres rien ne dure.
>
>   Tais-toi, tais-toi.
>   On n'aime qu'une fois.[18]

The emphasis is on the bachelor's embarrassment and the lady's self-deception and pathos. But in the lengthened version, number VIII of *Derniers Vers*, there is a distinctly new element added to the poem: the sense of the Romantic *manqué*, of failed opportunity on the bachelor's part.

> C'est la douceur des légendes, de l'âge d'or,
> Des légendes des Antigones,
> Douceur qui fait qu'on se demande:
> 'Quand donc cela se passait-il?'   (p. 302)

and

> Il n'y a pas là tant de quoi saigner?
>
> Saigner? moi pétri du plus pur limon de Cybèle!
> Moi qui lui eusse été dans tout l'art des Adams
> Des Edens aussi hyperboliquement fidèle
> Que l'est le Soleil chaque soir envers l'Occident![19]

That last grand gesture is ironic, but the question is asked, in effect, What was the nature of the relationship? 'La douceur des légendes' seems to hang over the affair despite the tendency to see it ironically. There is a delicate soupçon of genuine regret together with the view of the self as incapable of high romance, 'pétri du plus pur limon de Cybèle'. The first version of the poem takes up a stance of light mockery where the irony is directed entirely against the lady. The second adds the element that makes Eliot's poem such a complex and searching one – 'And should I have the right to smile?' In the first version the epigraph from *Hamlet* epitomizes the burden of the poem, which accuses the lady of immodesty. In the second version the epigraph is omitted. The speaker thinks of the future and tries to forget the past:

> (Oh! comme elle est maigrie!
> Que va-t-elle devenir?
> Durcissez, durcissez,
> Vous, caillots de souvenir!)[20]   (p. 301)

43

and looks forward to an epilogue rather like that in Eliot's poem, with its 'evening yellow and rose', 'cet épilogue sous couleur de couchant'. He seems to be cajoling the lady into coming to terms with both their failures. Laforgue has passed beyond Hamlet's self-regard and priggishness – and Laertes's in this case – and with a melancholy, Gallic shrug tries to get the lady to see and make light of the limitations and lost opportunities of both of them.

The echoes of Hamlet and Ophelia and the epigraphs from *Hamlet* play an integral part in Laforgue's recurring themes in all these poems. Partly, no doubt, they simply add an element of the mock-heroic, to make the poet's exploits all the more pathetic and absurd. But they also in themselves share the mood of the poems. It seems that Laforgue saw in Shakespeare's character a kind of mask for himself, a mask of the self-doubting hero whose relations with the heroine are marred by his fundamental doubts about all women, and about himself. Laforgue is struggling with some of the problems in which Hamlet was enmeshed, trying to solve them by turning them into comedy, bringing them under the playful mastery of his lightness of touch. For the problems are as much potentially comic as tragic. The comedy is implicit in *Hamlet* too, but there it serves to intensify the tragedy and make it more painful. In Laforgue the combination works in the opposite way: the tragic echoes give a flavour of melancholy to the comedy. Like J. Alfred Prufrock, Eliot's most Laforguian figure, Laforgue might well have said in the end, 'No! I am not Prince Hamlet, nor was meant to be.' But was Hamlet ever quite Hamlet either? 'He cannot *be* Hamlet', said Madariaga. It seems that Laforgue found a kind of *alter ego* in the mask of Hamlet, not simply a hero with which to contrast himself. Reading *Hamlet* seems to have helped him, I suggest, to see a seriousness as well as an absurdity in his predicament, and to take himself seriously as well as not too seriously. Hamlet's mind was one through which he could explore, and criticize, his own. Somewhere in Laforgue's mind was an idea of the truth, but in trying to express it he always stumbled, like the dancer of the Square of the Hypotenuse; so he made the fall a part of the act, indeed almost the whole act. But the fall would not have been so piquant if the pretensions it undermined had not been serious ones.

4

'Taint not thy mind'

T. S. Eliot

No! I am not Prince Hamlet, nor was meant to be;
Am an attendant lord, one that will do
To swell a progress, start a scene or two,
Advise the prince; no doubt, an easy tool,
Deferential, glad to be of use,
Politic, cautious, and meticulous;
Full of high sentence, but a bit obtuse;
At times, indeed, almost ridiculous –
Almost, at times, the Fool.[1]

But what did Prufrock think Hamlet was? One who did 'murder'
(if not 'create')? One who did 'disturb the Universe'? Certainly one
who had time for 'a hundred indecisions / And for a hundred visions
and revisions'. Hamlet can also 'bite off the matter with a smile':

— Denmark's a prison.
. . .
— We think not so my lord.
— Why then 'tis none to you.   (II.ii. 247, 252–3)

And Hamlet, unlike Prufrock, does roll the universe towards some
'overwhelming question' – 'To be or not to be'. Prufrock's Hamlet
is the hero, the romantic Hamlet primarily, the hero whom
Prufrock cannot be. But Hamlet himself has Prufrockian moments.
He could be said to have seen 'the moment of his greatness flicker'.
(And is he 'great' at the end of the play?) The footlights may be
said to 'throw his nerves in patterns' on the backcloth. He may not
'fast' (though Polonius says he does), but he 'weeps and prays'. He
is almost, at times, the Fool. He says at one point that Polonius
should be as old as he is 'if, like a crab, you could go backwards'.
He should, perhaps, have been 'a pair of ragged claws, scuttling

45

across the floors of silent seas'. There is here an implied comparison of himself with Polonius, which perhaps prompted Mallarmé's observation that Hamlet saw Polonius as 'the bundle of loquacious emptiness which he would later risk becoming in his turn, if he grew old'. He also shares with Polonius a predilection for bookish maxims.

Hamlet, then, was for Eliot in 1911 the romantic hero, but a particularly interesting romantic hero because his heroism seems to tend towards something very different, a Prufrockian lack of belief in himself. He is the romantic hero on the verge of becoming something else. 'No! I am not Prince Hamlet, nor was meant *to be.*' Putting the emphasis on that last verb, we can read the line as answering Hamlet's famous 'question'. And a distinguished modern critic, Salvador de Madariaga, has voiced the idea that Hamlet's problem was that he could not 'be', either. 'Hamlet can think Hamlet; he cannot *be* Hamlet.'[2] The points of contact between Hamlet and Eliot's *persona* are not simply points of contrast: the allusions bring Hamlet and Prufrock closer together, suggesting a Hamlet like Laforgue's, as well as on the surface differentiating them. In rejecting an identification with Hamlet, Prufrock is still thinking in romantic and heroic terms (only Prufrock would think of comparing himself with a hero in the first place). The poem is Eliot's critique of the vestiges of a literary romanticism in a modern mind, and he turns to Hamlet for an aptly ambiguous symbol of that romanticism.

After 'The Love Song of J. Alfred Prufrock' Eliot does not again use the failed romantic as a *persona*. And in writing on *Hamlet*, too, he becomes more detached and objective, and turns to the critical essay. In an essay of 1919, responding to J. M. Robertson's book, *The Problem of 'Hamlet'*, he elegantly sets aside the romantic concentration on Hamlet the character, and applauds the attempt to take account of the play as a whole.[3] It is a counterpart to the movement in his poetry away from 'personality' (of which there is still a lot in 'Prufrock'). He finds the play a failure precisely because it is too 'personal' – or rather because for him the personal emotion has not found an adequate form or 'objective correlative'. Where Eliot's theory may be questioned is in the way he transfers what he sees as Hamlet's emotional incoherence to Shakespeare: Hamlet is overwhelmed by emotion which he cannot understand, and *therefore* Shakespeare is too. The logic is clearly suspect. But the general point – that the play is not clear – may still be valid. Eliot's transference of Hamlet's feelings to Shakespeare, however, suggests that Eliot is still seeing the play as springing very directly from personal feeling. Eliot agrees with Robertson that the emotional centre of the play lies in a son's feelings about his mother's guilt, and this points to a strain which is, overwhelmingly, in the play. Where one may disagree with Eliot is over the question of whether the facts as presented are or are not an adequate expression of the feeling.

It has been pointed out that Eliot's formula here, whether or not applicable to *Hamlet*, does apply to his own case in *The Family Reunion*. Is Harry's generalized disgust at life adequatedly explored in the framework of the drama, with its conventional mystery element (Did she fall or was she pushed?)? It certainly seems that much of Harry's rather turgid gloom is not adequately accounted for by the 'facts' as presented. Is it some sin of the parents which accounts for Harry's dilemma, or his own sin, or 'The shadow of something behind our meagre childhood / Some origin of wretchedness'? The problem does not perhaps admit of adequate dramatic embodiment, especially in Eliot's terms.

Is Eliot then, in talking of *Hamlet*, transferring his own particular artistic problems on to Shakespeare, and hence falling – curiously enough – into the trap he sets out to avoid: the trap of filling a vacuum in the play with an idea drawn from the critic's own character or problems or creations? Eliot does not turn Hamlet into himself, as does Coleridge, or into a Werther, as does Goethe; but he turns *Hamlet* the play into an Eliotic art-problem.

Eliot is attempting to look at *Hamlet* in a detached and critical manner. But there is still this curious element of identification. And this is the more striking when we consider the similarities between *Hamlet* and Eliot's work in general: the prevalent physical disgust, the incandescent wit, the powerful expressions of despair, the cryptic allusiveness. *The Family Reunion* is linked in surprising ways to Eliot's diagnosis of *Hamlet*. Hamlet's disgust is at what he sees as his mother's guilt: her sin is the sin of sensuality and lovelessness (there in the swift forgetting of King Hamlet). Harry's disgust can also be seen as springing from his perception of lovelessness, between his parents and between himself and his wife. His disgust is hardly as focused as Hamlet's, and takes a different form, because it is a response to coldness, and a *lack* of physical feeling, rather than sensuality. It is a response to some void in childhood. This void is too simply symbolized by the disappearance of the hollow tree of his and Mary's memory, and too simply evoked by the glimpses of childhood memories of guarded looks and the whisperings of 'triumphant aunts'. The psychology, or the feint at psychological explanation, is also too simplified and leaves one with the feeling that the piece, for all its subtleties, is rather heavy-handed. Eliot has not, one could argue, found the right 'objective correlative' for the emotions he wanted to express.

The problem of the *Hamlet* essay and the problem of this play seem to fall together. Firstly Eliot diagnoses the *Hamlet* problem as we might diagnose that of the later play. Secondly there is a similarity between what Eliot sees as the central feeling of *Hamlet*, and what we can see as the central feeling of Eliot's play. Eliot has therefore not only turned *Hamlet* into an art-problem similar to his own, as I suggested, but has also alighted on precisely the 'theme' in *Hamlet* closest to his own personal and artistic concerns. Prufrock saw Hamlet romantically, just as he tried to see himself romantically. Eliot in 1919 sees *Hamlet* filled with preoccupations similar to his own and hampered by artistic problems he himself experienced in his own writing.

It is striking that the artist's and the critic's response to *Hamlet* seem in Eliot to be inseparable. And it is as an artist that Eliot has, I think, his most profound perception of *Hamlet*, and puts that perception to best creative use. In working out his own personal and poetic problems in *Four Quartets*, at a deeper level than in his plays, Eliot draws on the play in a way which shows how deeply it was involved in his own artistic inspiration, and in doing so gives us a new insight into the play.

But before looking at this later work, there are instances of earlier reference to *Hamlet* in the poetry which should be noted, for they show how from the first the play (together certainly which much other literature) impinged on Eliot's imagination. In 'A Game of Chess', the second section of *The Waste Land*, the talk in the pub modulates at the end into Ophelia's words:

HURRY UP PLEASE IT'S TIME
HURRY UP PLEASE IT'S TIME
Goonight Bill. Goonight Loo. Goonight May. Goonight.
Ta ta. Goonight, Goonight.
Good night, ladies, good night, sweet ladies, good night,
    good night.   (p. 42)

The effect aimed at is one of pathos. The melancholy behind the cheery pub conversation and the more sordid monologue of Lil's friend is suddenly brought out by this leap across three centuries into the atmosphere of a totally other world. At the same time we hear the voice of the poet himself, the whimsical and melancholy onlooker like the onlooker in the *Preludes*, murmuring the quotation to himself in slightly self-conscious irony. The effect does not for some reason seem to be as telling as many of the other effects in the poem. The irony is perhaps too easy, too much a matter of simple contrast between these 'vulgar' women and 'the sweet, the fair, the divine Ophelia', and suggested simply by the association of the words rather than any deeper similarity or contrast. Perhaps it is also because the whole sequence in the pub has too much a feeling of slightly snobbish pastiche (like the treatment of the Maid in Eliot's 'On the Eve: a Dialogue').[4] But whatever its success, the point of the allusion must lie partly in the contrast between the sordid affair hinted at by Lil's friend and the tragic breakdown of the love between Ophelia and Hamlet. Perhaps there is some further irony about the suppressed sexual longings which emerge in Ophelia's songs lingering behind this allusion, but it is not fully realized. One can only venture the point that the situation of Hamlet and Ophelia may perhaps associate itself in Eliot's mind with his distaste at the ways of modern love.

There are other 'echoes' of *Hamlet* which are probably unconscious or just fortuitous, but which suggest connections of subject and emotional preoccupation between the play and Eliot's poetry. In 'Gerontion' we have these lines:

      In the juvescence of the year
Came Christ the tiger

In depraved May, dogwood and chestnut, flowering judas.   (p. 21)

That sharp evocative paradox, 'depraved May', echoes the description of a Virginian springtime in *The Education of Henry Adams*.[5] But it is also curiously similar to Hamlet's

> 'A took my father grossly, full of bread,
> With all his crimes broad blown, as flush as May.   (III.iii. 80–1)

The feeling in both cases gets its force from the compression of the images of springtime and corruption, a compression that evokes a sweet, seductive corruptness, a rising of the sap tainted at the source, a dangerous sensuousness. It is there too in the Ghost's phrase about 'the blossom of my sin'. Sensual life is always felt to be dangerous in Eliot, one may recall. 'The ecstasy of the animals' in 'Marina' means 'death'. Like Webster, Eliot sometimes crawled between dry ribs to keep his metaphysics warm. Like both of them, Hamlet is much possessed with death and with the corruptions of sexuality. For these reasons if for no others, one might describe *Hamlet* as Shakespeare's most Eliotic play. In both the play and Eliot's poetry, particularly the early poetry, there is a similar mood of irony, bitterness, disgust, alleviated by wit and comedy; there are the same kinds of obsession, the same sense of a waste land, 'weary, stale, flat and unprofitable'. We have had Hamlet as Coleridge, and Hamlet as Werther, and should perhaps resist making Hamlet an Eliot. But there is still a striking series of parallels between play and poetry, the sense of a shared nexus of problems. Eliot too uses an antic disposition to help him make sense of the world: 'Hieronymo's mad again.' There is a sense of conflicting perspectives in *Hamlet*, as in *The Waste Land*, and a central consciousness for whom the world has lost its meaning. It comes to seem less and less coincidental that the climax of 'Little Gidding', indeed of *Four Quartets* as a whole, should be a meeting with a ghost.

Gerontion himself says: 'I have no ghosts.' His problem (unlike Hamlet's) is that he has lost touch with the moral values and injunctions of the past.

> I was neither at the hot gates
> Nor fought in the warm rain
> Nor knee deep in the salt marsh, heaving a cutlass,
> Bitten by flies, fought.   (p. 21)

Hamlet, too, never 'smote the sledded Polacks on the ice'; but he hears Horatio tell him of how King Hamlet did, and the first scene of the play is full of memories of the old king's military exploits. For Gerontion, the past is a confusing mass of jumbled echoes, odd names and enigmatic glimpses. It is richly unclear whether

> I that was near your heart was removed therefrom (p. 23)

refers to Christ, or a past lover, or both. For him there is no single voice saying 'Remember me.' Eliot's problem at this stage (for the expression of which Gerontion acts as a *persona*) is that the past is a chaotic mass of various traditions and memories, with no dominant tradition to act as a central inspiration. By the time he wrote *Ash Wednesday* Eliot was beginning, of course, to find that central tradition in Christianity. And if there is one figure who was the focus of that tradition for Eliot, and who became, in effect, Eliot's 'ghost', it was Dante. But the movement in that direction, away from fragmentary chaos towards the construction of 'something upon which to rejoice' (*Ash Wednesday*), also brought its dangers. The domination of a single tradition or mentor (whether King Hamlet, or Dante) could lead to self-righteous disdain of life, moral bullying, and a distaste for normal human feelings. History, for Hamlet as well as for Gerontion,

> deceives with whispering ambitions,
> Guides us by vanities. (p. 22)

And if we think of Hamlet's moral progress, from conscientious inaction to rash, morally suspect action, and finally to a *coup de grâce* executed in a tumult of chance events, we may find an extraordinarily apt commentary in Gerontion's words:

> Neither fear nor courage saves us. Unnatural vices
> Are fathered by our heroism. Virtues
> Are forced upon us by our impudent crimes. (p. 22)

'Gerontion' and *The Waste Land* occupy the same point in Eliot's artistic development that *Hamlet*, for all the differences of genre, occupies in Shakespeare's. All three works are complex, ambiguous, full of conflicting elements and styles and conflicting perspectives; all have the seeds in them of future works and future moral certainties, but as yet these are mingled with negative, destructive elements. All is in solution, in a state of potentiality. Each work is fragmented, imperfect.

The distaste for normality was one of the things Eliot had to contend with in his later poetry: to contain it so that it did not poison his perception of life; or better still to dispel it by seeing life in a new way. 'Taint not thy mind.' *Four Quartets* is a sustained exploration of the deepest sources of Eliot's hope and his despair. Its varying voices lighten its touch so that the gaucheries of *The Family Reunion* are never apparent, for there is always an ironic voice to alleviate and transform them if they threaten. The play makes an apt comparison because the same concerns (and often the same phrases) appear in it, but deprived of Eliot's voice. The details of childhood, so evocative in 'Burnt Norton', appear in the play simply as a few elements, baldly indicated, of the realistic story, and thus fail to achieve life and resonance. But in *Four Quartets* Eliot does succeed in employing glimpses of a remembered or imagined childhood to alleviate 'the burden of the mystery' of life and suffering. And his success in doing so is related to a changing perception of *Hamlet* which bears fine artistic fruit in 'Little Gidding'.

The way Eliot's feelings about *Hamlet* seem to relate to the theme of his own poetry might first be explored a little further. The disgust at sexuality in *The Waste Land* can be briefly recalled, and the preoccupation with dissolution and death in *Ash Wednesday*. But there is a deeper connection in the subject of relations between son and parents. Hamlet derives his dilemma from the injunction from his father's ghost and from his feelings about his mother. Harry in *The Family Reunion* derives his, ostensibly, from his own loveless marriage and his doubts about his parents' marriage – a suspicion of coldness in his mother, and an ignorance about his father. There is surely something fundamental here for our sense of Eliot's poetic problems, though there is no need to be simply biographical. What seems undeniable when one reads 'Burnt Norton' is that the sense of momentary reconciliation and illumination achieved in the first section of the poem seems to relate to the situation of the play. In the marvellous passage on the rose garden, the quick rhythms of childish excitement are followed by the awed moment of stilled, concentrated attention, and the visionary moment; there is a deep sense of reconciliation with lost presences, and a seeing into the life of things.

> Other echoes
> Inhabit the garden. Shall we follow?
> Quick, said the bird, find them, find them,
> Round the corner. Through the first gate,
> Into our first world, shall we follow
> The deception of the thrush? Into our first world.
> There they were, dignified, invisible,
> Moving without pressure, over the dead leaves,
> In the autumn heat, through the vibrant air,
> And the bird called, in response to
> The unheard music hidden in the shrubbery.
> And the unseen eyebeam crossed, for the roses
> Had the look of flowers that are looked at.
> There they were as our guests, accepted and accepting.
> So we moved, and they, in a formal pattern,
> Along the empty alley, into the box circle,
> To look down into the drained pool.
> Dry the pool, dry concrete, brown edged,
> And the pool was filled with water out of sunlight,
> And the lotos rose, quietly, quietly,
> The surface glittered out of heart of light,
> And they were behind us reflected in the pool.
> Then a cloud passed and the pool was empty.
> Go, said the bird, for the leaves were full of children,
> Hidden excitedly, containing laughter,
> Go, go, go, said the bird: human kind
> Cannot bear very much reality.   (pp. 117–18)

It would be intrusive to try and define too precisely who 'they', in this passage, are. But they are from 'our first world'. And we may remember these passages:

Agatha. Harry must often have remembered Wishwood –
The nursery tea, the school holiday,
The daring feats on the old pony,
And thought to creep back through the little door.
He will find a new Wishwood. Adaptation is hard.
. . .

Yes. I mean at Wishwood he will find another Harry.
The man who returns will have to meet
The boy who left. Round by the stables,
In the coach-house, in the orchard,
In the plantation, down the corridor
That led to the nursery, round the corner
Of the new wing, he will have to face him.   (Part I, scene 1)

53

Harry. It seems I shall get rid of nothing,
Of none of the shadows that I wanted to escape;
And at the same time, other memories,
Earlier, forgotten, begin to return
Out of my childhood. I can't explain.
But I thought I might escape from one life to another,
And it may all be one life, with no escape. (Part I, scene 2)

Agatha. I only looked through the little door
When the sun was shining on the rose-garden:
And heard in the distance tiny voices
And then a black raven flew over.
  . . .

Harry I was not there, you were not there, only our phantasms
And what did not happen is as true as what did happen,
O my dear, and you walked through the little door
And I ran to meet you in the rose-garden. (Part II, scene 2)

The rose-garden, the children's voices, the journey back 'into our
first world', of 'Burnt Norton', are clearly echoed in *The Family
Reunion*; but in the context of drama, with its specific characters and
story, they do not have the power which they have in the earlier
poem. One might compare also these lines of Harry's to Mary in Part
I, scene 2,

> I have spent many years in useless travel;
> You have stayed in England, yet you seem
> Like someone who comes from a very long distance,
> Or the distant waterfall in the forest,
> Inaccessible, half-heard.
> And I hear your voice as in the silence
> Between two storms, one hears the moderate usual noises
> In the grass and leaves, of life persisting,
> Which ordinarily pass unnoticed,

with these from 'Little Gidding',

> The voice of the hidden waterfall
> And the children in the apple-tree,
> Not known, because not looked for
> But heard, half-heard, in the stillness
> Between two waves of the sea. (p. 145)

What seems to have happened is that Eliot has transposed experience
which in the play he attempted to embody in terms of characters
and situations into the more symbolic medium of the poem –

T. S. Eliot

'symbolic' because there is no attempt to link it to a realistic context of specific imagined lives and relationships, but at the same time much more personal in its intensity. But to look at the play may give one some clues about the kind of experience out of which the poetry came. In the light of the play, 'they' in the 'Burnt Norton' passage come to seem like parental presences, from whom there has been some alienation, but with whom there is now, in the imagination, a kind of reconciliation:

> There they were as our guests, accepted and accepting.
> So we moved, and they, in a formal pattern. (p. 118)

Perhaps one should not be so specific: but at the least there is a sense of a burden lifted at the source of experience, an achieved reconciliation with previously alienated and oppressive presences. In 'Little Gidding' this is achieved again, this time at the level of more complex adult experience, in the meeting with the 'familiar compound ghost'. And here the influence of *Hamlet* again seems to be important. The meeting is a kind of extension of Hamlet's experience: for whereas he dies, tragically, in carrying out the Ghost's command, Eliot meets his ghost to learn the limits of its previous teaching. The ghost is 'some dead master' and at the same time all Eliot's dead masters. (Critics have seen the figure as Mallarmé, Milton, Dante, Dr Johnson and many more. One might add Shakespeare, and Eliot's Unitarian father.) He embodies, one might say, the whole spirit of authority, artistic example, ethical injunction, the commands of the spirit. And here these commands and teachings are felt to have something in them which needs *forgiveness*, as if, perhaps, in any authority of teacher over pupil, father over son, or one artist over another, there is an element of power, of a dangerous domination of mind over mind which may inhibit individual freedom and genuine individuality. Was it by following such injunctions that Eliot was led to 'things ill-done and done to others' harm / Which once you took for exercise of virtue'? The Ghost in *Hamlet* commands 'Remember me', and 'Revenge my foul and most unnatural murder'; the ghost in 'Little Gidding' enjoins forgetting, and forgiving.

> And he: 'I am not eager to rehearse
> My thought and theory which you have forgotten.
> These things have served their purpose; let them be.

55

So with your own, and pray they may be forgiven
By others, as I pray you to forgive
Both bad and good.   (p. 141)

'Both bad and good': it seems as if even good teaching – the exercise of that kind of power – has an element in it that needs to be forgiven. The commands of the Ghost in *Hamlet* are far from certainly good, but even if they are, they might still be seen in that way. And there are further ways in which echoes of *Hamlet* in the poem suggest that the connection is not just accidental. Hamlet names the Ghost, and confers on it an identity which until then had been in doubt: 'I'll call you father, King, Royal Dane!' So the speaker in Eliot's poem compels a recognition by his words:

So I assumed another part, and cried
And heard another's voice cry: 'What! are *you* here?'
Although we were not. I was still the same,
Knowing myself yet being someone other –
And he a face still forming; yet the words sufficed
To compel the recognition they preceded.   (p. 141)

But whereas Hamlet's collaboration in creating this identity leads to a tragic burden and death, the speaker's here leads to a reunion, a speech of strong pessimistic wisdom, and a final 'valediction'.

Hamlet cannot disentangle his sense of duty from the burden of disgust and rejection of life which are there in his first soliloquy and which the Ghost's narrative intensifies. Eliot in 'Little Gidding' achieves just such a disentanglement, by evoking the spirit of all his 'dead masters' and learning from it the limitations of its teaching and the need for the 'refining fire' (that fire, perhaps, which King Hamlet's Ghost says that he is enduring

Till the foul crimes done in my days of nature
Are burnt and purged away).   (I.v. 12–13)

After this Ghost's first appearance, Marcellus relates,

It faded on the crowing of the cock,   (I.i. 157)

which leads him to associate it with 'erring spirits'. And in its departure from Hamlet its last words are 'Remember me.' The departure of Eliot's ghost echoes Marcellus's line, but transforms the echo from something ominous to something strengthening. The

ghost leaves at the sounds of the first stirrings of city life after the
air-raid, fleeing from the modern urban reality. But its leaving is
dignified and far from guilty, and the sound of the horns also
suggests a kind of waking up from a dream, to a newly clarified
vision, as with the huntsmen's horns beautifully described in *A
Midsummer Night's Dream*. Its last words (or perhaps it is a gesture)
enjoin not remembrance but a 'vale' – 'Be valiant.' The effect is of
mystery, but also of awakening to a sober clarity of vision.

> The day was breaking. In the disfigured street
> He left me with a kind of valediction,
> And faded on the blowing of the horn.   (p. 142)

The progress of Eliot's engagement with *Hamlet* follows the progress
of his artistic development: from the romanticism and irony of
Prufrock's identification with the hero, through the more 'impersonal' critical view of the essay of 1919, to the profound creative
response to the play in 'Little Gidding'.This last is as important,
I suggest, as the creative response to *Pericles* in 'Marina'. In both
instances elements of Shakespeare's imaginative creation are assi-
milated and recreated in an entirely original way.

Prufrock could not 'be' Hamlet the hero: the terms of the
conception were wrong. But in 'Little Gidding' Eliot does achieve
a rare and fine sense of identity in his meeting with the ghost.

> I was still the same
> Knowing myself yet being someone other –
> And he a face still forming; yet the words sufficed
> To compel the recognition they preceded.   (p. 142)

The recognition compelled is both that of the ghost and that of the
speaker himself. We see the speaker in process of transformation.
Four Quartets moves beyond a tragic incoherence of self to achieve
a profound sense of wholeness.

Eliot has made brilliant creative use of *Hamlet*. He also, I think,
leads us to reconsider our views of the play itself. It shifts our
attention from Gertrude and 'a mother's guilt' where it is focused
in Eliot's essay, to the Ghost. The commands of ethical injunction,
of the spirit, are seen in the ambiguity that besets them when they
become involved with actual human motives and actions: that is

to say, not that they themselves are impure, but that in our experience they never present themselves in unambiguous purity and clarity. Bradley and many other critics have seen Hamlet's task as 'a sacred duty', but never was a sacred duty so hedged by doubts and ambiguities. Nor have many sacred duties led to so many 'things ill done and done to others harm' which the doer takes 'as exercise of virtue'.

5

'Methinks I see my father'
Joyce's *Ulysses*

Joyce's *Ulysses* is so full of allusions to *Hamlet*, and echoes of its language, that Joyce would seem to be the foremost exemplar of the creative use of the play in modern literature. But at the same time *Hamlet* is only one of many myths in *Ulysses*. We cannot say it provides the underlying legend for the story, since the *Odyssey* clearly outdoes it there. Moreover the allusions and echoes are so multiform, and point in such different directions, that it is difficult to argue that Joyce makes any *one* use of *Hamlet*. It is dangerously easy to move from a critical view of the subject to one that is merely annotatory. The allusions and their cross-connections are so labyrinthine that it is easy to get lost in the maze and begin to wonder if it has a pattern and a centre at all. Richard Ellmann has recently added another expert chart of Joyce country to his previous maps of the territory, the tracing of critical paths in *Ulysses on the Liffey*, and the vast Mercator's Projection of the *Life* of Joyce.[1] This map, *The Consciousness of Joyce*,[2] deals with the area most pertinent to the present subject: the area in Joyce's consciousness occupied by Homer, and Shakespeare, and finally some aspects of politics. The chapter on Shakespeare is virtually a chapter on *Hamlet*, and Professor Ellmann explores this particular maze with erudition and ingenuity. But whether he has reached a centre, or traced out the lines of the main path, is more questionable. He might reply that passages that lead nowhere are as interesting as those that go to the middle, or that Joyce was tracing the maze for its own sake and not simply to get to the centre. This may have some truth, but it makes things difficult for the non-Joycean. But can you give me some idea of the point of it all?, he is likely to ask. Can you show me that this net of allusions actually *catches* anything in the way of experience,

59

or of ideas; or (if you prefer), that when spread out and held up to the light, it reveals some coherent pattern? Are the allusions simply a literary game or do they reinforce or decorate some central subject of the book? Can you answer Edmund Wilson's criticism that Joyce's 'literariness' and elaboration were pedantic, and that the strength of the book lies much more in its evocation of the stuff of ordinary consciousness and Dublin life?[3] This chapter will try to keep these questions in mind while exploring the part *Hamlet* plays in *Ulysses*.

Joyce's 'theory' of *Hamlet* may by now be notorious, but it can be briefly sketched. He sees the play as directly autobiographical. Shakespeare is the Ghost, for Shakespeare was cuckolded by one of his brothers. The play marks the beginning of a preoccupation with sexual anguish in Shakespeare's work, which continues in *Othello* and *King Lear* and is finally erased by the spirit of reconciliation in the last plays. This 'autobiographical' view is built up out of a host of facts, half-facts, legends and conjectures, a kind of amalgam of history and speculation which appears to have been a staple element of popular Shakespeariana in Joyce's time. In itself, no one is probably likely now to take the theory seriously as a means of understanding the play. The question is, did Joyce take it seriously himself? He lectured on the play in Trieste in 1912–13. The lectures do not survive, but according to Professor Ellmann the newspaper reports 'appear to confirm' that they followed much the same course as Stephen Dedalus's theory in *Ulysses*. Stephen himself does not seem to take his ideas seriously, or at least, he does not *believe* in his theory.

—You are a delusion, said roundly John Eglinton to Stephen. You have brought us all this way to show us a French triangle. Do you believe your own theory?

—No, said Stephen promptly.[4]

And yet most of the long scene in the National Library in Dublin is taken up with the discussion of *Hamlet*. What then is its significance? It could be partly that Stephen is simply mocking contemporary scholarship; in the spirit, say, of Oscar Wilde's memorable question 'Are the critics of *Hamlet* mad or are they just pretending to be?' But this in itself would hardly justify the extended discussion of the theory in the novel. The clues to why it is there lie rather, I suggest, in the following passage. It is necessary not only to extract Stephen's theory, but to pay attention to the tone of his discussion and its dramatic context.

—Come, he [John Eglinton] said. Let us hear what you have to say of Richard and Edmund. You kept them for the last, didn't you?

—In asking you to remember those two noble kinsmen nuncle Richie and nuncle Edmund, Stephen answered, I feel I am asking too much perhaps.

A brother is as easily forgotten as an umbrella.

Lapwing.

Where is your brother? Apothecaries' hall. My whetstone. Him, then Cranly, Mulligan: now these. Speech, speech. But Act. Act Speech. They mock to try you. Act. Be acted on.

Lapwing.

I am tired of my voice, the voice of Esau. My kingdom for a drink.

On.

—You will say those names were already in the chronicles from which he took the stuff of his plays. Why did he take them rather than others? Richard, a whoreson crookback, misbegotten, makes love to a widowed Ann (what's in a name?), woos and wins her, a whoreson merry widow. Richard the conqueror, third brother, came after William the conquered. The other four acts of that play hang limply from that first. Of all his kings Richard is the only king unshielded by Shakespeare's reverence, the angel of the world. Why is the underplot of *King Lear* in which Edmund figures lifted out of Sidney's *Arcadia* and spatchcocked on to a Celtic legend older than history?

—That was Will's way, John Eglinton defended. We should not now combine a Norse saga with an excerpt from a novel by George Meredith. *Que voulez-vous?* Moore would say. He puts Bohemia on the seacoast and makes Ulysses quote Aristotle.

—Why? Stephen answered himself. Because the theme of the false or the usurping or the adulterous brother or all three in one is to Shakespeare, what the poor is not, always with him. The note of banishment, banishment from the heart, banishment from the home, sounds uninterruptedly from *The Two Gentlemen of Verona* onward till Prospero breaks his staff, buries it certain fathoms in the earth and drowns his book. It doubles itself in the middle of his life, reflects itself in another, repeats itself, protasis, epitasis, catastasis, catastrophe. It repeats itself again when he is near the grave, when his married daughter Susan, chip of the old block, is accused of adultery. But it was the original sin that darkened his understanding, weakened his will and left in him a strong inclination to evil. The words are those of my lords bishops of Maynooth: an original sin and, like original sin, committed by another in whose sin he too has sinned. It is between the lines of his last written words, it is petrified on his tombstone under which her four bones are not to be laid. Age has not withered it. Beauty and peace have not done it away. It is in infinite variety everywhere in the world he has created, in *Much Ado About Nothing*, twice in *As You Like It*, in *The Tempest*, in *Hamlet*, in *Measure for Measure*, and in all the other plays which I have not read.

He laughed to free his mind from his mind's bondage.   (pp. 271–2)

The whole tone of Stephen here seems to be one of weary flippancy. He is weary of his friends whom he doubts; he is tired of his own voice. The wit in his conversation seems strained. The theory of *Hamlet* is one which obsesses him but which he does not believe: the last sentence of the passage seems crucial: 'He laughed to free himself of his mind's bondage.' The theory is a tortured and tortuous one; it suggests that Shakespeare writes the play in a spirit of revenge and as a means of revenge. Joyce follows the legend that Shakespeare played the part of the Ghost. In addressing Hamlet he is also addressing his own son Hamnet (1585–96).

We can hardly take this seriously because it rests on no solid evidence. The important thing is how it reflects Stephen's own consciousness, for Stephen often sees himself as Hamlet, and his friends and relations as other characters in the play.

In the book's first episode ('Telemachus' was the heading Joyce gave to Stuart Gilbert), Haines says to Stephen that the Martello tower and its cliffs remind him of Elsinore, '*That beetles o'er his base into the sea*, isn't it?' 'In the bright silent instant Stephen saw his own image in cheap dusty motley against their gay attires.' 'It's a colourful tale', Haines says. And a moment later, 'I read a theological interpretation somewhere, he said bemused. The Father and Son idea. The son striving to be atoned with the father.' It is only a small clue, but Haines's idea has a bearing on one of the main themes of the novel – Stephen's alienation from his father[5] and all the other paternalistic authorities that surround him, the church, his teachers, the English government. His meeting with Bloom can also be seen as a kind of atonement with a father-figure, a representative of the 'ordinary' humanity of Dublin against which he has felt himself in such fierce opposition.

It has been suggested too that Buck Mulligan can be seen as a kind of Claudius in his role as usurper.[6] He takes the keys of the Martello tower, and the episode ends with the picture of the sensual Mulligan swimming out at sea, and Stephen's thought: 'usurper'. More generally and significantly perhaps, since this is the impression we form of him from the episode as a whole, Mulligan is a kind of usurper of Stephen's role as the bard and wit of his generation. He shares Stephen's satirical contempt for his age, but without Stephen's humility. He pushes himself forward, interrupting the others, flaunting his arch ebullience. He seems to try and share Stephen's consciousness and to outdo it, to get in on Stephen's act and upstage him at the same time. There is a kind of anxious desire to ally himself with Stephen against the world, but he lacks Stephen's independence of mind. When Stephen offends Haines with a joke about money, Mulligan is indignant, but he ends up being over-urgently comradely:

— You put your hoof in it now. What did you say that for?
— Well? Stephen said. The problem is to get money. From whom? From the milkwoman or from him. It's a toss up. I think.
—I blow him out about you, Buck Mulligan said, and then you come along with your lousy leer and your gloomy jesuit jibes.
— I see little hope, Stephen said, from her or from him.
Buck Mulligan sighed tragically, and laid his hand on Stephen's arm.
— From me, Kinch, he said.
In a suddenly changed tone he added:
— To tell you God's truth I think you're right. Damn all else they are good for. Why don't you play them as I do? To hell with them all. Let us get out of the kip. (p. 19)

An ambience of allusions to *Hamlet* is established in this first section, and as it develops through the novel one can see, I think, the broad outline of its significance. Stephen feels himself the inheritor of an indistinct obligation to Ireland – to write creatively for the race. He is surrounded at once by the ghosts of the past (the Church, his mother's ghost, the memories of Parnell and nationalist heroism; and, as a writer, the shade of Shakespeare), and the usurpers of the present (Buck Mulligan, the usurper of his poetic role; the English king and government, the usurpers of the rule of Ireland). From the Church he inherits a consciousness of sin, particularly of the sins of the flesh (which we have seen more fully in *A Portrait of the Artist as a Young Man*), and this is intensified by his feelings of guilt at not having taken communion when bidden to do so by his dying mother. This consciousness is the most important element: it leads him to a contempt for ordinary human life, which he must overcome if he is to become an artist, for an

63

artist must work with the stuff of life. His feelings about Shakespeare and *Hamlet* are closely involved with these preoccupations. Hamlet inherits a task from the ghost of his father which seems at times to be a sacred duty. But the Ghost's narration of his murder and the Queen's adultery also confirms Hamlet in his disillusionment with women and his disgust at this too solid flesh, and it is this disillusionment and disgust which poison his mind and impede his action.

Already then there are important parallels between Stephen's situation and Hamlet's. But the fundamental question that torments Stephen is, What was Shakespare's primary creative motive in writing the play? Out of what personal experience did it spring? Is it a play written in a spirit of revenge, and as a kind of revenge? We are told that Joyce sometimes saw his own writing as a way of getting back at his enemies. We are also told that Joyce was once troubled by the malicious slander by a former friend that Nora had been unfaithful to him. And on another occasion Nora herself told Joyce that an Italian friend of Joyce's had tried to seduce her. An honest writer in this position, dealing with his contemporaries and writing from personal experience, would be acutely aware of the difficulties here of getting over his private grudges and of writing in a spirit of disinterestedness. Was *Hamlet* written in a spirit of personal obsession which would vitiate its artistic greatness? Was one of the greatest of Shakespeare's tragedies, and the most perplexing and fascinating of them, written in a spirit of hatred? Was the greatest of English writers, the great ghost whose presence hovered over Joyce the writer, an inspiration and a challenge, in fact poisoned in this play at the centre of his career, by the spirit of jealousy and revenge? The question would strike at the centre of Joyce's beliefs in Shakespeare, in himself, in the art of literature and human nature. In struggling with the problem of *Hamlet*, Stephen Dedalus (and Joyce) are struggling with the problem of their creativity.

It is at this point that the role of Bloom becomes important. Bloom typifies ordinary, decent, vulgar, pathetic, unheroic man, his lack of heroism and his comic pathos emphasized by his impotence. He is married to a hedonistic woman of great sexual energy, who has cuckolded him countless times; and he is forced to accept this with a kind of pained embarrassment. In bringing Stephen and Bloom together at the end of the novel, Joyce is trying to embody an idea of the artist's awakening consciousness of 'ordinary' life, and the ordinary man's unheroic human qualities. Molly Bloom's soliloquy, too, is a brilliant attempt to identify completely with a woman's experience, to see her life utterly from the inside – the life of a woman who could easily have been a Gertrude. Joyce is immersing himself in unheroic life in a way that shows a profound effort of imaginative creation, and discovers values and human feelings alien to the exalted idealistic spirit of Stephen in the earlier part of the novel. And a part of this exploration of the consciousnesses of Bloom and Molly is an exploration of the non-literary man's honourable if confused sense of the necessity of art.

For *Hamlet* is not only important as a part of Stephen's consciousness, but also as a part of Bloom's. The play serves as a constant source of trite moral reflections for Bloom, but as a kind of touchstone of sanity none the less. In Bloom's mind we have an alternative sense of *Hamlet* which implicitly criticizes Stephen's and puts it into perspective.

In the graveyard at the funeral of Paddy Dignam, Bloom's thoughts run, in the spirit of the gravediggers' in *Hamlet*, on the physical facts of death and dissolution. It is an episode in which morbid reflections – which everybody has – are deprived of their morbidity by a lively curiosity and a zestful apprehension of physical facts. Bloom does not vaunt these thoughts (like Hamlet); they are simply running through his head. They show the instinctive curiosity of the human mind and its ability to face and cope with the physical facts of death. For Bloom's mind is not fixed on the unpleasant facts; in its spontaneous and natural progression it is master of them and floats them in a medium of free-ranging thoughts.

He has seen a fair share go under in his time, lying around him field after field. Holy fields. More room if they buried him standing. Sitting or kneeling you couldn't. Standing? His head might come up some day above ground in a landslip with his head pointing. All honeycombed the ground must be: oblong cells. And very neat he keeps it too, trim grass and edgings. His garden Major Gamble calls Mount Jerome. Well so it is. Ought to be flowers of sleep. Chinese cemeteries with giant poppies growing produce the best opium Mastiansky told me. The Botanic gardens are just over there. It's the blood sinking in the earth gives new life. Same idea those jews they said killed the christian boy. Every man his price. Well preserved fat corpse gentleman, epicure, invaluable for fruit garden. A bargain. By carcass of William Wilkinson, auditor and accountant, lately deceased, three pounds thirteen and six. With thanks.

I daresay the soil would be quite fat with corpse manure, bones, flesh, nails, charnelhouses. Dreadful. Turning green and pink, decomposing. Rot quick in damp earth. The lean old ones tougher. Then a kind of tallowy a kind of cheesy. Then begin to get black, treacle oozing out of them. Then dried up. Deathmoths. Of course the cells or whatever they are go on living. Changing about. Live for ever practically. Nothing to feed on feed on themselves.

But they must breed a devil of a lot of maggots. Soil must be simply swirling with them. Your head it simply swurls. Those pretty seaside gurls. He looks cheerful enough over it. Gives him a sense of power seeing all the others go under first. Wonder how he looks at life. Cracking his jokes too; warms the cockles of his heart. The one about the bulletin. Spurgeon went to heaven 4 a.m. this morning. 11 p.m. (closing time). Not arrived yet. Peter. The dead themselves the men anyhow would like to hear an odd joke or the women to know what's in fashion. A juicy pear or ladies' punch, hot, strong and sweet. Keep out the damp. You must laugh sometimes so better do it that way. Gravediggers in *Hamlet*. Shows the profound knowledge of the human heart. Daren't joke about the dead for two years at least. *De mortuis nil nisi prius*. Go out of mourning first. Hard to imagine his funeral. Seems a sort of joke. Read your own obituary notice they say you live longer. Gives you second wind. New lease of life.

(pp. 136–8)

It is quite natural that Bloom should think of *Hamlet* here; no obtrusive 'allusion' is being forced on us. But the thought also reminds us of how Joyce seems to be recreating the robust humour of Shakespeare's gravediggers (and how in the play itself that spirit counters the melancholy brooding, the' considering too curiously', of Hamlet in that scene). In Stephen's theory of the play Joyce draws on the darker side of *Hamlet* to express the consciousness of the young protagonist. In Bloom we are reminded of the parts of the play which are not Hamlet and the Ghost, reminded of its currents of centrality and sanity. Bloom's actual memories of the play are usually of the tritest kind, but this too is part of the point. Shakespeare is not the unique preserve of intellectuals like Stephen but is remembered also by men like Bloom. 'Music hath charms. Quotations every day of the year. To be or not to be. Wisdom while you wait'. Banal reflections, but the underlying sentiments are not worthless. The phrases of the play mingle with his other thoughts and help to give them a certain dimension, a universality. And whereas Stephen associates the play with his more anxious thoughts, Bloom finds in Shakespeare's verse a harmonious solemnity. Stephen thinks of the Ghost with anxiety: Bloom remembers rather the harmonious effects of Shakespeare's language at a moment when the Ghost appears. Watching the gulls from O'Connell Bridge:

He threw down among them a crumpled paper ball. Elijah thirtytwo feet per sec is com. Not a bit. The ball bobbed unheeded on the wake of swells, floated under by the bridge piers. Not such damn fools. Also the day I threw that stale cake out of the Erin's King picked it up in the wake fifty yards astern. Live by their wits. They wheeled, flapping.

> The hungry famished gull
> Flaps o'er the waters dull.

That is how poets write, the similar sounds. But then Shakespeare has no rhymes: blank verse. The flow of the language it is. The thoughts. Solemn.

> Hamlet, I am thy father's spirit
> Doomed for a certain time to walk the earth.   (p. 192)

The recollection of *Hamlet* by Bloom may also point to Bloom's role in the novel as Stephen's discovered father and mentor. It blends with a number of other echoes, and suggests how utterly different minds can meet on a common ground of a shared language and literary tradition. The first time Stephen sees Bloom is during the discussion of *Hamlet* in the National Library – a glimpse, as Bloom tiptoes in to borrow a book. The first time Bloom sees Stephen is from the window of the creaking carriage on the way to Paddy Dignam's funeral, 'a lithe young man, clad in mourning, a wide hat'. These glimpses, a part of the subtly visual, almost cinematic, aspect of Joyce's technique, foreshadow the meeting to come. There is a kind of 'prophetic soul' in the novel which allows the reader these premonitions.

But Stephen and Bloom meet for the first time in the phantasmo-goric drama of the 'Circe' episode, in Bella's brothel. Bloom's sexual humiliation is acted out and, I think, purged in the comic fantasy. Into this web of dreams are woven threads from that anguished drama of sexual jealousy and revenge which haunts Stephen's mind. Stephen's mother appears to him, ghastly and rotting in the accoutrements of the grave, and brings to a climax his whole sense of guilt about her; Paddy Dignam's ghost appears, and like King Hamlet's calls from underground. (Unlike him, however, he announces he died from natural causes!) Fragments of the tragic suffering of Shakespeare's play are thrown into the potpourri and evaporate into the steam of comic fantasy. Stephen had earlier concocted his wild theories about Ann Hathaway with echoes of Ophelia, *Venus and Adonis, Macbeth*, and Goldsmith.

If others have their will Ann hath a way. By cock she was to blame. She put the comether on him, sweet and twentysix. The grey-eyed goddess who bends over the boy Adonis, stooping to conquer, as prologue to the swelling act, a bold faced Stratford wench who tumbles in the cornfield a love younger than herself.   (p. 244)

Virag Bloom in the 'Circe' episode echoes the same song with more sinister intent, as he taunts Bloom lasciviously about the charms of Bella's whores.

(*Cynically, his weasel teeth bared, draws down his left eye with a finger and barks hoarsely.*) Hoax! Beware of the flapper and bogus mournful. Lily of the alley. All possess bachelor's button discovered by Rualdus Colombus. Tumble her. Columble her. Chameleon.   (p. 629)

The repressed sexual instincts which emerge in Ophelia's songs are here echoed in this *Walpurgisnacht* of the erotic. The disturbed speculations of Stephen's theory of *Hamlet* are glimpsed in fragments. When Bloom is tormented by Bella about Molly's infidelity and his impotence, he is suddenly cast in the role of Hamlet himself, alienated from society, vowing revenge and being called to by a ghostly voice:

Bella.   They will violate the secrets of your bottom drawer. Pages will be torn from your handbook of astronomy to make them pipeswills. And they will spit in your ten shilling brass fender from Hampton and Leedom's.
Bloom.   Ten and six. The act of low scoundrels. Let me go. I will return, I will prove...
A voice. Swear!
(*Bloom clenches his fists and crawls forward, a bowie knife between his teeth*).
                                                                                    (p. 654)

Bloom is brought 'closer' to Stephen, in terms of the thematic movement of the novel, by being cast for a moment in the role of vengeful romantic hero. At the same time the role is ridiculed. Hamlet is here identified with Bloom rather than Stephen, and the vengefulness, posturing and self-pity potentially in the Hamlet role are here brought to light and rendered comically. The role of Hamlet is transferred from the serious and troubled Stephen to the comic and pathetic Bloom: Joyce's troubled obsession with *Hamlet* is being erased by comedy. He is able to see what one might call the Hamlet-instinct even in a man like Bloom, which is a gain in perspective, even humility. Joyce is looking into the roots of his own romantic sense of persecution, superiority and hostility, by seeing them as elements too in the most unheroic life. He is also looking deep into his own sexual perplexities and finding them embodied and exemplified as much in Bloom as in Stephen. In this way he renders them in a comic perspective, and in the end purges them by a *reductio ad absurdum*. Stephen was beginning to imagine, in his theory of *Hamlet*, a Shakespeare consumed with sexual jealousy (to the point of bequeathing it to his son) and spurred to write by vengefulness. In the crazy world of Nighttown this troubling speculation blooms into the comic fantasy which is its proper medium. Stephen and Bloom, together, look into 'The mirror up to nature' and see

(...*The face of William Shakespeare, beardless, appears there, rigid in facial paralysis, crowned by the reflection of the reindeer antlered hatrack in the hall.*) *Shakespeare* (*in dignified ventriloquy*). 'Tis the loud laugh bespeaks the vacant mind. (*To Bloom*) Thou thoughtest as how thou wastest invisible. Gaze. (*He crows with a black capon's laugh*) Iagogo! How my old fellowchokit his Thursday momum. Iagogogo!   (p. 671)

It is the final evaporation of Stephen's theory of Shakespeare as cuckold. His mind is cleared of it not by disproving it (you cannot disprove a fantasy) but by letting it run its course in the dreamworld of the protagonists. Shakespeare's obsession in this scene leaves him spluttering a garbled version of Hamlet's bitter taunt (via the Player Queen): 'Weda seca whokilla farst'. His face merges with that of Martin Cunningham, who looks on impassively at his merry widow. Gertrude is metamorphosed into Mrs Cunningham in her kimono, 'sidling and bowing, twisting Japanesily'. And Stephen's obsession with *Hamlet, ou Le Distrait, pièce de Shakespeare* (the title Mallarmé once saw in a French theatre) expires in farce.

69

The spirit of Bloom leads Stephen in the direction of purging his guilt and the perverse elements in his idealism; and the fate of Stephen's theory of *Hamlet*, and the counterpoise of Bloom's sense of the play, illustrate one aspect of that process. In the last section of the novel, Bloom emerges as a kind of Aristotelian mind turning outwards to the objective facts of the world, and Stephen as a kind of Platonic and artistic mind (as in Raphael's picture of *The School of Athens*, where Plato points vigorously upward to the heavens and Aristotle gestures in a broad, generous gesture to the expanse of life below). Bloom's mind looks outward to problems of society: however trivial and confused and intermittent his wider consciousness is (his ideas of muncipal reform, for instance), it is still the confused engagement of an essentially decent mind with the world. He is blessedly free from morbid scruples and Hamlet's self-destructiveness. (When he talks of a sailor making a quietus 'with a bare bodkin' it is characteristic that *he* is not thinking of suicide.)

We do not, it is true, see a great deal of Stephen's reactions to Bloom. But what we do see suggests that Stephen becomes aware through him of other traditions, a sense of ghosts and injunctions from a wider sphere than the one he has hitherto experienced. When Bloom chants from the Hebrew, Stephen 'heard in a profound ancient and unfamiliar melody the accumulation of the past', while Bloom 'saw in a quick young male familiar form the predestination of a future' (pp. 807–8). It is a kind of rediscovery of the past and the future – the sense of tradition – in terms independent of family pieties and merely local social ties. Stephen (and Joyce too) had to escape from a restricted sense of tradition and obligation, in relation both to literature and society. In purging himself of his obsession with Shakespeare he is also freeing his own creative genuis, freeing it so that it can become itself more genuinely Shakespearian. The various figures of authority mingle here, and one of them is Stephen's father. It is only by freeing himself from him, as from Shakespeare, that Stephen can hope to create and genuinely further the tradition. Once he has freed himself, a kind of reconciliation is possible, as in this moment in the Nighttown episode, in which Stephen calls to his father in cries like Hamlet's at I.v. 116:

Stephen. No, I flew, My foes beneath me. And ever shall be. World without end. (*He cries*) Pater! Free!

70

Bloom. I say, look...

Stephen. Break my spirit, will he? *O merde alors!* (*He cries, his vulture talons sharpened*) Hola! Hillyho! (*Simon Dedalus's voice hilloes in answer, somewhat sleepy but ready*)

Simon. That's all right. (*He swoops uncertainly through the air, wheeling, uttering cries of heartening, on strong ponderous buzzard wings*) Ho, boy! Are you going to win?...Head up! Keep our flag flying!

(p. 674)

Stephen's meeting with Bloom sums up his whole tendency towards a wider view of life, escaping his past not by an act of destruction but an act of sympathy. A few pages after the above passage Stephen cries out, striking his head, 'But it is in here I must kill the priest and the king.' His rebellious attitude to the Catholic Church on one hand and the English government on the other is still very much alive. But he realizes that the forces of oppression are as much within himself as outside. His own mind is still dominated by inherited prejudices. Bloom represents an ordinary humanity, and in his Jewishness another cultural tradition, both of which Joyce has to learn (by writing *Ulysses*, say, or by going to Paris). Even the self-critical violence of that cry does not represent what Stephen and Joyce really had to do, which was not to become politically subversive, but to create (and unseat inherited prejudices that way). The cry itself shows Stephen's political ineptness in a small but important way, for it leads directly to his imbroglio with the English soldiers. And this in turn leads to the moment at which he and Bloom are finally brought together, as Bloom comes forward to help him out of the scrape. The incident is small but the symbolic implications are large. Bloom rescues Stephen, in the broadest sense, from his self-destructive fighting talk and would-be heroic posturings. And this too is what his immersion in the lives of Bloom and Molly and the other Dubliners of *Ulysses* did for Joyce. The meeting of Stephen and Bloom symbolizes that moment of recognition for Joyce: the novel is both about that process, and the result of it. To sink himself into the life of Bloom enables Joyce to create, to act. Is it entirely accidental that what is probably the last echo of *Hamlet* in the novel should come when Bloom and Stephen hover on the threshold of Bloom's house as Bloom fumbles for the key? Hamlet's dilemma has often been seen to focus itself in his great question, 'To be or not to be'; and Stephen's fate is finely poised at this symbolic moment of entering Bloom's house.

> What were the alternatives before the, premeditatedly (respectively) and inadvertently, keyless couple?
> To enter or not to enter. To knock or not to knock.   (p. 779)

The artist has to transcend the limitations of his own personal experience in order to create. Joyce does so in his ability in *Ulysses* to enter into the life of Leopold Bloom. Stephen's theory of *Hamlet*, so limitingly biographical, suggested a Shakespeare bound in the toils of personal obsession and unable to escape from them. But Shakespeare's greatness is just that he *can* imagine so many different kinds of life, so much so that his own life is almost invisible in his works. Joyce, Shakespeare, or any artist, must go out from the self through the imagination, in order to find his artistic self. This is what Stephen comes to recognize in the 'Circe' episode; in a passage where, with a fine ironic touch, the external world breaks in even while he is theorizing about it.

> *Stephen* (*Abruptly*). What went forth to the ends of the world to traverse not itself. God, the sun, Shakespeare, a commercial traveller, having traversed in reality itself, becomes that self. Wait a moment. Wait a second. Damn that fellow's noise in the street. Self which it itself was ineluctably preconditioned to become. *Ecco!*   (p. 623)

Stephen's theory of *Hamlet* is initially a paradigm of his whole theory of art. But it is one which has to yield to the larger sense of life of Joyce himself, as he discovers it – 'traversing not himself' – in the writing of *Ulysses*.

Hamlet would have needed either to 'conceive the plan and let the religious doubt take it from him', or (better still) to carry out the revenge 'demoniacally' and to 'collapse within himself' in 'the religious experience'. (This latter alternative, incidentally, sounds interestingly comparable to *Macbeth*.) But what, I think, is especially pertinent to the play as it stands is Kierkegaard's feeling that it has an ambiguous status, somewhere between a religious drama and something else.

The point is that Kierkegaard seems to feel that Shakespeare does not provide enough in the way of religious postulates to make Hamlet's doubt and hesitation unambiguously religious, and that if he had, the subject would perhaps not have been suitable for drama at all. But without such postulates Hamlet simply becomes a 'morbid' figure:

If Shakespeare will not give Hamlet religious postulates which conspire against him to produce religious doubt (wherewith the drama should properly end) then Hamlet is essentially a victim of morbid reserve and the aesthetic demands a comic interpretation.

The idea of morbidity reminds one of interpretations like those of Wilson Knight which stress this aspect of Hamlet's character; and the mention of comedy reminds one that there are, indeed, comic elements in the play, like the cellarage-scene which, as Coleridge noted, give a peculiar kind of grotesquerie and intensity to certain moments of the tragedy. But what is most important, I think, is that Kierkegaard seems to feel that the play hovers between the states of religious drama and this kind of comedy of morbidity, and that he is not sure quite how to interpret it. 'If [Hamlet] is conceived religiously', he writes further on, 'his scruples have great interest, they insure that he is a religious hero.' 'How does Shakespeare conceive him?' is our next obvious question, but Kierkegaard does not seem finally to decide. Nevertheless, his view of a kind of ambiguity between 'religious scruple' and 'morbid reserve', as well as between a 'religious' drama where the hero's conflict is within himself and an 'aesthetic' one where it is essentially external, is, I think, very suggestive. It leads to points about *Hamlet* which we find Kierkegaard considering elsewhere, and to a view of the play which we can derive from these considerations. This view focuses on just this ambiguity in Hamlet's scruples and hesitations: are they those

91

of a morbid figure or those of a religious hero? Is his secretiveness a courageous independence necessitated by the circumstances of the Ghost's revelation and the fear of discovery, or is it a perversity springing from a kind of guilt?

In an essay entitled 'Kierkegaard and Hamlet', Denis de Rougemont draws a parallel between the tragedy of Hamlet and the course of Kierkegaard's life.[2] The parallel hangs on the idea that both the fictional and the real man had 'hidden' vocations to rid Denmark of a usurper: in Hamlet's case Claudius, and in Kierkegaard's the false, conventional Christianity of the Church of his day. Both heroes have to hide this task behind 'indirections', masks and 'antic dispositions'. The parallel is, naturally, speculative and ingenious, and may not do much more in the end than demonstrate once again how varied the applications of *Hamlet* as an allegory or symbol can be. But de Rougemont sees the cases diverging over the matter of what Kierkegaard calls the 'objective uncertainty' of genuine vocation. In Kierkegaard's case this uncertainty is central: he cannot 'prove' the rightness of his vocation but has to believe in it as a matter of faith, which means of course that it is also subject to doubt. But, says de Rougemont, in Hamlet's case there is no such 'objective uncertainty'. 'Hamlet *knows* exactly what he has to do; he must kill the usurper and avenge the murdered king. His aim is unequivocal and his role is clearly defined.' Now I would suggest that Hamlet's aim is not so unequivocal. He may say he knows what he has to do, but his actions throughout the play suggest the case is not so simple as this. And there is precisely that 'objective uncertainty' (which Hamlet himself voices) about the Ghost's revelation, which de Rougemont denies. The details of the play which support this idea will be explored in due course in this chapter and in Part 2, but here the important thing is to suggest that it is just this 'objective uncertainty' about his task and his own state of mind which Kierkegaard sees in Hamlet, and which is related to his use of Hamlet as an illustration, elsewhere, of the idea of 'dread'.

Kierkegaard describes 'dread' or *angst* (the Danish word conveys pain as well as fear) as, to quote his translator Walter Lowrie, 'a presentiment of something which is "nothing"'; it is 'the next day' and a 'fighting against the future';[3] a premonition of freedom, or of the possibility of good and evil. In children 'dread' is seen as a seeking after adventure, 'a thirst for the prodigious and the mysterious'. In biblical terms it is an awareness of sin – not a knowledge of good and evil, but 'the whole reality of knowledge projected in dread as the immense nothingness of ignorance'. The prohibition about the tree of knowledge awakens dread in Adam, because it awakens the possibility of freedom, of 'being able'. He is not yet guilty, but he is aware of the possibility of guilt.

In his journal entry for 17 January 1837, Kierkegaard suggests that it is the quality of dread that gives force to Hamlet's tragedy:

If something is really to become depressing the foreboding that there is something wrong must first of all develop in the midst of the most favourable circumstances, one does not become conscious oneself of anything so wrong; but it must lie in the family history, then the all-consuming power of inherited sin shows itself, which can grow into despair and have far more terrible effects than that fact whereby the truth of the foreboding is confirmed. That is why Hamlet is so tragic.[4]

About Shakespeare's play there is one inaccuracy here. Hamlet's foreboding does not develop 'in the most favourable circumstances' but directly in response to his mother's remarriage. But the passage is still suggestive in relation to the play. If we take 'the family history' to refer in Hamlet's case to the immediate history of the remarriage (and not some more distant history, in which case it would be irrelevant to the play), Kierkegaard's analysis is to the point. And Hamlet's foreboding and sense of disgust in his first soliloquy does seem to reveal a sense of taint in his own nature, perhaps of some 'inherited sin'. We are conscious, as L. C. Knights says, of a particular quality in the speaker in Hamlet's first soliloquy, a vibration in the way of expressing his feelings, which attracts our attention to his own state of mind, not simply to the facts he is describing.[5] And it is possible to see in Hamlet's subsequent behaviour a greater relation to this original self-disgust than to the 'confirmation' of his suspicions by the revelations of the Ghost. The Ghost indeed confirms Hamlet's original feelings in many ways (accepting for the moment that we are to trust the Ghost), but the fundamental and weariness and dread are already there: 'It is not, nor it cannot come to good.'

His behaviour towards Ophelia, for instance, cannot be simply accounted for by what his mother has done and what the Ghost has told him. A certain kind of mind would have been quite able to separate his mother's actions from his view of woman's nature in general ('What has she done, prince, that can soil Ophelia?', as Ulysses might have said had he been in this play). In the nunnery-scene Hamlet's doubts are also as much of himself as of Ophelia: 'What should such fellows as I do, crawling between earth and heaven?' This fundamental doubt is not related specifically to his inaction by Hamlet himself, but our accumulated impression must be that there is a connection, and that he does not act because of some self-doubt.

In *The Concept of Dread* Kierkegaard cites Hamlet once in relation to the idea of 'shut-upness' (p. 114). This state is one of self-enclosure caused by fear of self-revelation, and specifically by what Kierke-gaard describes as evil's 'dread of the good', or 'the demoniacal'. He contrasts this with 'reserve', which can be described as 'a pact with the good', and cites Shakespeare's Brutus and Prince Hal, who kept their real selves hidden in order to carry out a good act which in the end does reveal itself. This 'reserve' is 'shut up' with a great idea, whereas the demoniacal is shut up with only itself. The latter speaks in monologues: it seems to reveal but merely mystifies. This is the most subtle form of 'shut-upness', and Kierkegaard almost seems to impute this kind to himself. To reveal the inner workings of this state from his own experience would be impossible. 'Here I essay only to give everything "an understanding but no tongue"', as the shut-up Hamlet said warningly to his two friends' (p. 114).

This quotation makes explicit certain strains in the book which might well already have suggested Hamlet to the reader. This 'shut-upness', its monologues and mystifications, might very well describe Hamlet in his long self-communings, his cryptic utterances to Rosencrantz and Guildenstern, or to Polonius and Ophelia. We do not even know how much he tells Horatio of the basic 'facts' of 'the circumstances of my father's death'. Madariaga says that Hamlet talks only to himself.

Elsewhere in his journals and papers Kierkegaard uses Hamlet as an illustration in various ways. But in each of them his view is generally counter-romantic and suggests a mysterious hiddenness in Hamlet's character. He finds him 'morbidly reflective' and expresses his incredulity that Goethe 'has taken such great pains to

94

adhere to Hamlet'.[6] Yet in another place he approves of Goethe's image of the tree planted in the flower vase for Hamlet's task and the way it shatters him, and seems (like so many other writers) to identify himself with Hamlet here. Hamlet is an example of the intellectual 'genius' who knows speculatively of the truth, but is existentially below the rank of the 'apostle' because he cannot 'become' the truth subjectively.[7] In the *Concluding Unscientific Postcript* Kierkegaard criticizes Roetscher's view of the play for failing to recognize (theoretically at least) that Hamlet's decision to act comes not as a logical result of his reflections, but from a break with reflection; 'Reflection can be halted only by a leap.' In reflection the individual becomes 'objective' to himself and 'loses the decisiveness inherent in subjectivity'.[8] In all this Kierkegaard is seeing Hamlet as the type of the existential hero who cannot resolve the conflict between action and suffering and the conflict between action and thought. He illustrates Kierkegaard's argument that the human individual essentially experiences conflict and division, and that any Hegelian notion of a 'higher unity' where all oppositions are resolved is an abstraction of the mind which cannot be true for the subjective individual. As he says in one of his journal entries: 'Personality will for all eternity protest against the idea that absolute contrasts can be mediated...for all eternity it will repeat its immortal dilemma: to be or not to be – that is the question.'[9]

This immortal dilemma means also that Hamlet's character never resolves itself into the simple hero. Nor can his dilemma be fully explained. Kierkegaard has an interesting comment on the last scene of the play, which perhaps he slightly misreads but not in a way which disqualifies his point. Presumably remembering Hamlet's eagerness that Horatio should stay alive to tell his story, he comments: 'His sorrow, almost to despair, is that no one will ever come to know his life.' Hamlet has had a 'single idea' but has 'concealed it in the form of a deception'. But such a man must be consistent, must never 'secretly provide people with an explanation', must, 'after his death continue to be the riddle he was in life, for precisely this is the epigrammatic-judicial nerve of his life'.[10] In *Authority and Revelation* Kierkegaard discusses the same idea, and regards Hamlet as radically weakening at the end of the play by wanting the recognition of the world, and seems to regard this lapse as throwing doubt on Hamlet's character earlier in the play: 'But if Hamlet became softened at death, he could also have talked in his lifetime, that is, let the whole thing go.'[11] This suggests another point, which is that Hamlet's action in killing the King is based on information given to him alone, from a source (the Ghost) which cannot be corroborated – that it is virtually a purely 'inner' conviction. We the audience may have heard the Ghost but nobody else has. And it is not clear how much Hamlet has told Horatio, or how much Horatio credits what he has been told. Hamlet's conviction is a secret one which cannot be made public, which is what interests Kierkegaard about it. Hamlet's anxiety for his story to be told suggests to Kierkegaard a weakening of conviction (to which one might add Hamlet's speech in v.ii, in which he seems to be casting about for motivation; see below, p. 176). It is an anxiety to 'cover himself' which brings one back to the idea of dread, the dread of what final moral significance the action of killing the king will have.

This brings me back to my quotation from the journal of 1837, and to another remark Kierkegaard made in Volume I of *Either/Or*. There he writes: 'Hamlet is deeply tragic because he *suspects* his mother's guilt.'[12] As I suggested with the first quotation, it is here we can see the nub of Kierkegaard's view of the play. Hamlet's suspicion that there is something wrong grows into an awareness of 'the all-consuming power of inherited sin' and of a taint in his own nature. Hamlet's own suspicions are also the cause of his own self-doubt, for what if they proceed from his own mind, and his imagination *is* 'as foul as vulcan's smithy'? Is Hamlet's 'shut-upness', then, to return to that idea from *The Concept of Dread*, that of the demoniac who dreads a revelation because he dreads the good; or is it that of a Brutus or a Prince Hal, that is to say a 'pact with the good' which would be adulterated by any appeal to 'the world'? It is an ambiguity which is precisely that of dread, the premonition of the possibility of good and evil.

Hamlet could therefore be described as a tragedy of dread. And here one might remark on a feature of its structure which makes it unique among the tragedies: the fact that the hero's main action, the action to which the play is leading, does not come until the last scene. In *Macbeth* the hero is seduced – by the witches, by himself, and by his wife – into the decisive action that determines his fate, in the first Act. For a brief moment he is in a state of dread, hovering above the abyss of possibility:

> This supernatural soliciting
> Cannot be ill, cannot be good. If ill,
> Why hath it given me earnest of success,
> Commencing in a truth? I am Thane of Cawdor:
> If good, why do I yield to that suggestion
> Whose horrid image doth unfix my hair
> And make my seated heart knock at my ribs,
> Against the use of nature? Present fears
> Are less than horrible imaginings.
> My thought, whose murder yet is but fantastical,
> Shakes so my single state of man that function
> Is smothered in surmise, and nothing is
> But what is not.   (I.iii. 130–42)

Compare Kierkegaard's description of dread:

It speaks of being in dread of nothing...He who through dread becomes guilty is innocent, for it was not himself but dread, an alien power, which lay hold of him, a power he did not love but dreaded – and yet he is guilty, for he sank in the dread which he loved even while he feared it.[13]

Similarly, when Kierkegaard describes dread as 'an antipathetic sympathy and a sympathetic antipathy', the paradox is like that of Macbeth's attitude (to the weather or the battle) when we first see him: 'So fair and foul a day I have not seen'.

But this dread ends for Macbeth the moment he 'bends up each corporal agent' for the murder of Duncan. After that we see the tragic consequences of the guilt of a great man. In *King Lear* the rush towards the precipitation of the tragedy is even swifter. Lear is set on a wilful course the moment the play opens; there is no moment for dread (except perhaps in Cordelia). In *Othello* the case is closer to *Hamlet*. Othello does not murder Desdemona until the last Act of the play. But this terrible crime was building up long before. In III.iii comes the decisive change in Othello. His moment of dread lies in the moment he *entertains* Iago's thoughts of jealousy, and he is quickly drawn from dread of the worst to a belief in it, and then to the plunge into guilt. In these other three tragedies the time sequence differs considerably, but in each of them there is, at a certain point, a guilty act, preceded (except in the case of Lear) by a period of dread. Something similar could be said of Brutus's

97

tragedy in *Julius Caesar*, so close in many ways to Macbeth's. He too
is describing dread when he says:

> Since Cassius first did whet me against Caesar,
> I have not slept.
> Between the acting of a dreadful thing
> And the first motion, all the interim is
> Like a phantasma, or a hideous dream.
> The genius and the mortal instruments
> Are then in council, and the state of man,
> Like to a little kingdom, suffers then
> The nature of an insurrection.   (ii.i. 61–9)

But in his case the nature of the tragedy is questionable. We can
hardly see him as we see Macbeth, for he believes the murder of
Caesar is honourable. Kierkegaard saw Brutus as a good man, an
example of 'reserve' whose secrecy or 'shut-upness' is 'a pact with
the good'.

The uniqueness of *Hamlet* consists in this: that the moment of
dread lasts the length of the play. Hamlet is never finally resolved
on action; rather he gives in fatalistically to the course of events.
Even when he returns from England there is no resolution in his
mind, no calm acceptance of action, only an acceptance of death.
As he says to Horatio just before going off to the duel, 'But thou
wouldst not think how ill all's here about my heart.' The feeling of
dread is still there. The whole of *Hamlet* could be described as an
exploration of this state.

Dread is fear of the future and its unknown contents. And in
Hamlet, as in no other tragedy, this fear of the future is the staple
element of the dramatic atmosphere:

> – Who's there?
> – Nay, answer me. Stand and unfold yourself.

Against the natural order of events, it is the newcomer, the relief,
who challenges the soldier at his post. Who's there, in the darkness?
He knows someone should be there, but is it who he thinks? Even
ordinary expectation is troubled and upset. The opening words of
Hamlet establish this mood. The new watch is on edge; the old is
deeply melancholy: ''Tis bitter cold, / And I am sick at heart.'
Heart-sickness, that deep, groundless unhappiness which the Eliza-

bethans called melancholy, broods in the hearts of all the men in
this first scene; groundless, that is, but for the one premonition, as
yet uncertain, that all is not well: the reports of the 'thing' that has
appeared. What will happen tonight? It is the future which broods
over them, and dread of the future.

The Ghost appears suddenly as the soldiers and Horatio are all
gathered round Marcellus to hear the story of its first appearance.
In a brilliant stroke of dramaturgy, as the mind is relaxed from its
strained anticipation of the future, and has a moment's respite
looking into the past, *then* comes the apparition. But it does not
speak. And the explanation of its significance is again postponed into
the future, to a solution by young Hamlet – 'This spirit, dumb to
us, will speak to him.'

But Hamlet is already filled with a dread of his own. His first
soliloquy is full of weariness and disgust at the present: but it is a
prophetic dread that he ends with, a feeling that he must shut up
within himself:

> It is not, nor it cannot come to good.
> But break my heart, for I must hold my tongue. (I.ii. 158–9)

When he hears from Horatio and Marcellus it is like a confirmation
of his forebodings. His excitement mounts

> – Armed, say you?
> – Armed, my lord.
> – From top to toe?
> –   My lord, from head to foot.   (ll. 226–8)

And his conclusion is already couched in the terms of dread: he fears
the worst not just of what the Ghost will say, but of the Ghost itself:

> If it assume my noble father's person,
> I'll speak to it though hell itself should gape
> And bid me hold my peace.   (ll. 244–6)

The next appearance of the Ghost also comes at a moment of
lowered tension, when Hamlet is in the middle of his disquisition
on 'the vicious mole of nature'. Then, what will happen if he follows
the Ghost?

> What if it tempt you toward the flood, my lord,
> Or to the dreadful summit of the cliff

That beetles o'er his base into the sea,
And there assume some other horrible form,
Which might deprive your sovereignty of reason
And draw you into madness?   (i.iv. 69–74)

Fear of the future, of the unknown, of what will happen, grips Horatio too.

The Ghost confirms the melancholy forebodings in Hamlet's mind,

O my prophetic soul!
My uncle?   (i.v. 40–1)

but the confirmation does not remove his dread. For what is this Ghost, and what does it portend? At the end of ii.ii Hamlet is still not resolved on this.

The spirit that I have seen
May be a devil, and the devil hath power
T' assume a pleasing shape, yea, and perhaps
Out of my weakness and my melancholy,
As he is very potent with such spirits,
Abuses me to damn me.   (ii.ii. 610–15)

He still has to catch the King's conscience to confirm the Ghost's narration: the future is still dark, and holds the possibility of Hamlet's damnation.

For the ultimate dread is dread of death. It is this that dominates Hamlet's mind in his great soliloquy.

To die, to sleep –
No more – and by a sleep to say we end
The heartache, and the thousand natural shocks
That flesh is heir to! 'Tis a consummation
Devoutly to be wished. To die, to sleep –
To sleep – perchance to dream: ay, there's the rub,
For in that sleep of death what dreams may come
When we have shuffled off this mortal coil,
Must give us pause.
. . .

Who would fardels bear,
To grunt and sweat under a weary life,
But that the dread of something after death,
That undiscovered country, from whose bourn
No traveller returns, puzzles the will,

100

And makes us rather bear the ills we have,
Than fly to others which we know not of?

(iii.i. 60–8, 76–82)

The dread of something after death – this is what Hamlet's dread
of the future culminates in. 'To sleep, perchance to dream' – and
Hamlet has 'bad dreams'. The Ghost seems to be forgotten – as if
it does not associate itself at once with thoughts of the afterlife,
because it is still too doubtful and untrustworthy an apparition. The
speech continues, '*Thus* conscience doth make cowards of us all',
either the conscience that tells us to do right, or just the consciousness
of death; but in either reading it is associated with, springs directly
from, that 'dread of something after death'. 'The native hue of
resolution is sicklied o'er' – not so much with conscience as such,
or thinking too much, as Coleridge saw it – but with a conscience
about what comes after death. 'The pale cast of thought' is not just
any thought, but the thought of death, of that unavoidable future
state, which the mind dreads.

If the Ghost's story is confirmed by the play shown to the King,
is the dread then removed – the fear of being cozened by the devil,
abused and damned? Hamlet says the Ghost is an honest Ghost. But
he does not proceed and act on that assumption. Before he goes off
to see the Queen he expresses a feeling of vengefulness, but a rather
overblown and theoretical one. He also still associates revenge with
evil:

'Tis now the very witching time of night,
When churchyards yawn, and hell itself breathes out
Contagion to this world. Now could I drink hot blood
And do such bitter business as the day
Would quake to look on.   (iii.ii. 396–400)

The dread has been replaced by an exaggerated bloodthirstiness
which does not seem to go very deep – almost what Kierkegaard
describes as 'a thirst for the prodigious and mysterious' that he
associates with children.

In his interview with the Queen Hamlet is carried away from
thoughts of vengeance by the intensity of his desire to castigate his
mother with his words, mixed with a genuine desire to reform her.
His killing of Polonius is sudden, casual, and his reaction to the

murder is callous. He seems at this point in the play to be caught up in a whirl of activity which is at times nearly hysterical. At the end of iii.iv he is caught up in the delight of plotting against Rosencrantz and Guildenstern: 'O, 'tis most sweet / When in one line two crafts directly meet.' Dread has for the time being got lost in the rush of events and plotting – but plotting that bears no direct relation to Hamlet's main task or burden.

When Hamlet returns from England in v.i, the rush of events is past and he seem to have gained a kind of equilibrium. But his mind still runs on death, and in the graveyard he shows a kind of bitter, flippant nihilism. Dread of death seems here to have evaporated into a weary fatalism. It is in this spirit that he accepts Osric's invitation to the duel. One has to call it fatalism because, as Bradley says, a belief in Providence has to be allied to a determination to carry out the will of Providence, and this Hamlet does not show. In 'Not a whit, we defy augury' he shows he has rather given up thinking of the future than come to any assured conviction about it. The dialogue that precedes this speech gives us his state of mind

– You will lose this wager, my lord.
– I do not think so. Since he went into France I have been in continual practice. I shall win at the odds. *But thou wouldst not think how ill all's here about my heart.* But it is no matter.
– Nay, good my lord –
– It is but foolery, but it is such a kind of gaingiving as would perhaps trouble a woman
– If your mind dislike anything, obey it. (v.ii. 210–18)

I have emphasized by italics what seems to me a crucial line, a statement from the heart. Hamlet's mind does dislike something, and it seems to be more than just a suspicion that there is something suspect in the duel. That would not make him feel ill about his heart. It is something deeper than that, the feeling of dread. The shrugging disclaimer, 'it is such a kind of gaingiving as would perhaps trouble a woman', is more than flippant. Kierkegaard says that the feminine nature has an especial capacity for dread. It must be that Hamlet has not come to terms with himself or his burden: he is unable to confront the future with faith or certainty.

Hamlet kills the King in a fit of anger. Nothing is solved of what most deeply perplexes him. He leaves Horatio to work things out, and tell his story, feeling that otherwise he leaves behind him a wounded name. How much weight should we give to Fortinbras's last speech?

> Let four captains
> Bear Hamlet like a soldier to the stage,
> *For he was likely, had he been put on,*
> *To have proved most royal.* (v.ii. 396–9)

I have emphasized again a perplexing statement. Fortinbras does not know what we know, but the irony may be more than dramatic. Who, one might ask, has ever been 'put on' like Hamlet?[14] Has not Hamlet proved 'most royal'? Perhaps Fortinbras's speech is meant to make us stop and reflect. Has Hamlet ever really been brought to the point of *decisive* action, action that is resolved and which resolves? Has he not rather held back from action, *to the very end*, and only struck when it was unavoidable, when sudden anger and rashness makes him forget himself and rush at the King? The killing of Claudius solves nothing and precipitates nothing. Hamlet has received his death-wound before he strikes the blow. It is almost a posthumous act. It solves nothing because we do not feel it is *resolved* in Hamlet's mind, in which case it would be the culmination of a moral progression. It precipitates nothing because the play is over. The play ends looking into the future, not the future of the other tragedies where some kind of social order will be re-established or punishment meted out (though we hardly pay much attention to this), but a future where all which has hitherto been mysterious will be explained, by Horatio. Hamlet has reached no decisive action which would confirm or disprove his feelings of dread about himself. Macbeth does so act, and learns the consequences of his nature; so does Brutus; so do Othello and Lear, though by then it is too late for them to learn anything. Hamlet goes to his death in a state in which all is ill about his heart but is never clarified by action. He would seem to be the only tragic hero who has regularly been regarded as innocent. It has been said, and it seems a powerful truth, that the tragic hero is always wrong. But is Hamlet generally seen to be wrong? Hamlet is the tragic hero who hovers on the edge of tragedy, peering at its abyss in a state of dread, but never resolving to leap.

All the other Shakespearian tragic heroes *become guilty*, though it is a tragic guilt and our feeling about it must be complex, and different in each case. But Hamlet has generally either been thought not guilty at all (by Coleridge, Bradley, Dowden *et al.*), or guilty from the very beginning (most notably by Wilson Knight and Madariaga, the first finding him infected by a kind of 'death-infection', the second by a complete egotism). Neither of these opposing classes of view turns on the question of whether it is right or wrong to kill the King – quite correctly, since the issue is not debated in the play. They turn on how we judge Hamlet's soul *in toto*, scarcely with reference to the action of killing the King. Either that action is the precipitate of Hamlet's sense of duty, or of his egoism, or self-abandonment, or murderous nature, or whatever. Nor can we see the moment of killing Polonius as the decisive one: it is an accident, unpremeditated. However relevant it may be in assessing Hamlet's character, or to the movement of the plot, it is not a *turning-point* in Hamlet's moral development, like Macbeth's killing of Duncan, or Lear's banishment of Cordelia, or Othello's murder of Desdemona.

So there is no decisive tragic 'action' in *Hamlet*. For the killing of the King in the last scene is not decisive; the nature of the action remains ambiguous and 'decides' nothing. It is brought about merely by a mixture of chance and Claudius's machinations. Hamlet has already received his death-wound when he kills the King, and he strikes in a spirit of anger and self-defence, not in a spirit of justice or even a simple spirit of revenge. The whole emphasis of the play is on the doubts and vacillations, the 'accidental judgements, casual slaughters', and the hero's questioning of himself; on the time before the soul reveals itself in action, the time when it becomes aware of *possibility* – the equal possibility of good and evil – and holds back from the step that will commit it to one or the other, fascinated and appalled at once; the state of being which Kierkegaard described as dread.

Kierkegaard alludes only briefly to *Hamlet*, to further his own arguments. But *The Concept of Dread* as a whole, and Kierkegaard's observations in 'A Side Glance' and elsewhere, throw light back on the play, and on the other tragedies. They lead us to reconsider the whole status of *Hamlet* as a tragedy, and to distinguish it decisively from those other plays. We may remember that *Hamlet* is the first of the great tragedies and that it seems to mark a point between the freer spirit of the comedies, the analytical bitterness of *Troilus and Cressida*, and the greater finality of the later tragedies.[15] It is the moment when Shakespeare first gazes at the tragic paradox, expanded into a whole play. He takes the moment of dread which we see briefly in two other plays – in the trepidation of Macbeth on meeting the witches or the obsession of Brutus as he gazes at the possibility of killing Caesar – and makes it his central subject. In *Hamlet* the hero is poised for almost five acts in front of his great action. His inaction is not caused by ethical debate – revenge versus Christianity for instance – and certainly not by external forces. It is caused by something he cannot fathom. He passes over the idea that it might spring from 'bestial oblivion' or from (what Coleridge seized on) 'some craven scruple / Of thinking too precisely on the event'. For in the end, '*I do not know / Why yet I live to say, "This thing's to do."*' For all his penetrating thoughts he is ignorant of his own nature, and of the quality of it which would determine the value of his action. The play is the tragedy of what Kierkegaard describes as 'the whole reality of knowledge projected in dread as the immense nothingness of ignorance'.[16] But if Hamlet does not act decisively, is he a tragic hero at all? Not, I think, in the way the other Shakespearian tragic heroes are. Rather, it is a paradoxical play: one might, to describe it, adapt Donne's paradox in 'The Litanie',

> For some
> Not to be martyrs is a martyrdom,

and say that, for Hamlet, not to be a tragic hero is a tragedy.

8

'Bad dreams'
Franz Kafka

There is a reference to *Hamlet* in Kafka's diary entry for 29 September 1915, among a number of other remarks. The entry for the day reads:

All sorts of vague resolves. That much I can do successfully. By chance I caught sight on Ferdinandstrasse of a picture not entirely unconnected with them. A poor sketch of a frescoe. Under it a Czech proverb, something like: Though dazzled you desert the wine-cup for the maid, you shall soon come back the wiser.

Slept badly, miserably, tormenting headaches in the morning, but a free day.

Many dreams. A combination of Maschner the director and Pinisker the servant appeared. Firm red cheeks waxed black beard, thick unruly hair.

At one time I used to think: Nothing will ever destroy you, not this tough, clear, really empty head; you will never, either unwittingly or in pain, screw up your eyes, wrinkle your brow, twitch your hands, you will never be able to do more than act such a role.

How could Fortinbras say that Hamlet had prov'd most royally? [*sic*]

In the afternoon I couldn't keep myself from reading what I had written yesterday, 'yesterday's filth'; didn't do any harm though.[1]

Fortinbras did not, of course, quite say that Hamlet *had proved* most royally. What he said was

> For he was likely, had he been put on,
> To have proved most royal.   (v.ii. 398–9)

For Fortinbras (who did not yet know Hamlet's story), Hamlet, since he had not become a warrior or a king, had not been put to the test. But it is still a curious sentence in the last speech of the play, with undertones of retrospective dramatic irony beneath the formal tribute. I am told Kafka's German here is ambiguous; but it raises the question: did Shakespeare intend this tribute to carry unironic weight? Did Hamlet prove royal in what he *did* do? Kafka's remark reminds us that the tribute is not a straightforward one, and raises the whole question of how we should see Hamlet.

The remark is also interesting in its relation to the other remarks in the day's entry. It seems not unreasonable to look for some connecting train of thought, or at least an association of ideas. Out of what complex of ideas or feelings does the remark about Hamlet spring? The context does suggest that we can associate Kafka's thoughts about Hamlet with his thoughts about himself. 'All sorts of vague resolves. That much I can do successfully' – Hamlet might have said precisely this. 'Slept badly...Many dreams' – Hamlet slept badly and had 'bad dreams'. 'You will never be able to do more than act such a role' – Hamlet too is an actor who tries to induce in himself the appropriate feelings after watching the player deliver the Priam speech, and who rants histrionically over Ophelia's grave. There is just something stagey about him from the first as he enters in his 'inky cloak'. And his speech to the queen,

> 'Tis not alone my inky cloak, good mother,
> Nor customary suits of solemn black,
> Nor windy suspiration of forced breath...   (I.ii. 77–9)

makes a great display of outward behaviour while all the while saying, 'But I have that within which passes show.' Can Hamlet ever *be* Hamlet? I come back again to Madariaga's phrase. And it is just this problem of being, of reality, that Kafka is concerned with in his diary entry. What if the anguish he experiences is not *real*, if it is based on phantoms, on some contingent psychic condition, which makes it merely delusory, rather than a confrontation with something profound in human nature? Similarly, what if Hamlet's condition is simply a psychological special case? One might also suggest that the diary entry prompts thoughts associated with Kafka's and Hamlet's attitudes to women (the Czech proverb); and in the dream of the combination of the director and servant, an idea of a dual identity of Kafka and his father, or Hamlet and the Ghost.

The parallels between Kafka and Hamlet seem to me worth considering in spite of the obvious anomaly of comparing a fictional with a historical figure, and the objection that a large number of writers and thinkers have at one time or other seen themselves as

Hamlet. As Hazlitt said, 'It is *we* who are Hamlet'; and Edward Thomas wrote (with a nice irony): 'I suppose most men think *Hamlet* was written for them, but I *know* he was written for me!'[2] Essays have been written making close comparisons between Baudelaire and Hamlet, and G. Wilson Knight has found, almost literally it would seem, a reincarnation of Hamlet in the figure of Byron.[3] In many ways this kind of comparison seems of doubtful intellectual value: what, one might ask, is it trying to prove? Such enquiries may have a passing or incidental interest, an element of the 'Isn't it curious?', but one wonders what in the end can be *done* with them. If they are said to illustrate yet again how universal the 'character' of Hamlet is, and how his predicament can be seen cropping up again and again in real life (particularly the lives of 'intellectuals'), well, we may feel that it is unnecessary to multiply examples. But to look at *Hamlet* in the light of Kafka has, I hope, a more specific point: for it seems to me that it gives us an entrée into a modern sense of the play, into certain aspects of its tone and atmosphere and of its subject.

To begin with an example from the play's first lines:

> – Who's there?
> – Nay, answer me. Stand and unfold yourself.

That is entirely Kafkaesque. The new sentry hears a noise; he challenges; the challenge is thrown back at him. Ordinary expectations are foiled, we are suddenly aware of a new perspective which quite controverts our initial one. The moment is similar, in a compressed form, to the events at the beginning of *The Trial*, where Joseph K.'s perspective is immediately (and comically) altered by the reaction of the men who have come to arrest him:

'Who are you?' asked K., half raising himself in bed. But the man ignored the question, as though his appearance needed no explanation and merely said: 'Did you ring?'[4]

Question is answered by question, as challenge was by challenge. In the soldiers' case the new perspective is immediately comprehensible as it is not in Joseph K.'s, but the sudden shift is the same. The moment in *The Trial* epitomizes the process ('der Prozess') whereby Joseph K. finds himself in the midst of an alien world to the absurdity of which he gradually has to adjust himself; a process which is the essence of both the spiritual significance and the comedy of the story. The first two lines of *Hamlet* can also, as I have suggested, be seen as an epitome of a play in which the hero flings a question to a ghost ('What may this mean?') and has in turn to unfold himself. As in Kafka this is a play about perspective, in which *how we see* the characters and situation is both the critical problem and the subject. Kafka's works have been described as being all of them about the problem of interpretation: we could, I suggest, describe *Hamlet* in precisely the same way. Like Kafka's work, *Hamlet* seems to be a riddle in which the main critical problem is to find the key. But we may go further and say that, as with Kafka, the subject of the play itself *is* the problem of finding that key, and it is more the dramatization of that problem that matters, than the possibility that there is a right reading, a right perspective which will suddenly solve the enigma.

Before looking further at Kafka's work and the Kafkaesque in *Hamlet* it would be best to begin with some of the fundamental elements of Kafka's own character and predicament, and to suggest relations with those of Hamlet which will prepare the way for my argument that reading Kafka can help us to understand *Hamlet*. The two primary elements are: the sense of guilt connected with sex, and Kafka's relation with his father.

Kafka's sense of guilt about sex is evident throughout his diaries and his work in general. It was the main factor in his inability to marry – though bound up with a number of other factors. In a balance sheet on marriage and bachelorhood he once drew up in a notebook, he put as an advantage in the bachelor column 'I remain pure.'[5] He tells a story of a sexual encounter with a lower-class girl in which some small thing she said to him left him with a lasting disgust. But the problem (of course) went further back. In 'Letter to his Father' Kafka tells the story of a conversation he had with his father at about the age of sixteen.[6] The adolescent boy was airing his new-found knowledge or partial knowledge to his father, partly because, Kafka says, it was a pleasure to him to talk about it, partly 'out of curiosity', and partly 'in order to avenge myself on the two of you for something or other'. His father replied something about how he 'could give me some advice about how to go in for these

109

things without danger'. Kafka admits that it was perhaps just such an answer that he, 'with the pruriency of a child overfed with meat and all good things', was looking for. But still the reply cut his moral being to the quick. It was the first direct instruction bearing on actual life that he had received from his father. And its real meaning he describes as follows: 'What you were advising me to do was, after all, in your opinion, and still far more, in my opinion at that time, the filthiest thing possible.' And two sentences later he goes on: 'The main thing was, rather, that you yourself remained above your own advice, a married man, a pure man, exalted above these things.' In a much later conversation, when Kafka was thirty-six, his father wounded him in a similar way, though then, he reflects, it could hardly harm him any more. It was a conversation in which his father showed exasperation at his son's recent engagement, and more or less expressed surprise that a man of his age didn't just go off to the brothel and have done with it. 'If you're frightened, I'll go along with you myself.' And his mother seemed, he felt, to show her agreement by picking something up from the table and silently leaving the room.

I cite these painful examples to show something of what lies behind the experience of sexuality as we find it in Kafka's stories and novels: the tawdry weekly routine of Joseph K. before his arrest, and his voracious, emotionally meagre and spiritually baffling encounters with the women in the course of the novel; the squalid beginnings of K.'s encounter with Frieda in *The Castle* and her perplexing and ambivalent role in relation to K.'s progress thereafter; and the haunting significance of Amalia's story with its revelation of the depravity of a castle official and what I take to be its symbolization of the mysterious non-moral element in the most human and central of instincts. 'Lies behind' is deliberately vague, for I am far from believing that the biographical details, even if one could be sure of having the full truth about them, would in any way explain or account for Kafka's art.

The last examples show how closely Kafka's father was involved even in this aspect of Kafka's psychology: somewhere in this relation lies I think the root of Kafka's predicament. The story of Kafka's relations with his father generally is continued everywhere in Kafka's notebooks, diaries, and indirectly in his works themselves.

Kafka once said that all his works were about the struggle to escape from his father. Of course, if they were *only*, or even mainly, this, they would not have the universal significance they do. For Kafka's relations with his father are the only local psychological aspect of a dilemma that was infinitely more far reaching: the dilemma of man's relation with God.

For Kafka's relationship with his father was only the first – albeit psychologically the most formative – example of the predicament of Kafka's relation with the idea, or perhaps one should say the fact, of moral and spiritual authority. It is this great subject that informs (it can be ventured) *all* his work, from an early story like 'The Judgement' to his last novel *The Castle*. The tyrannical or godlike (which? that is the question) father/judge in 'The Judgement'; the family and the employer in 'Metamorphosis'; the old and the new governors and their penal systems in 'In the Penal Colony'; the shadowy hierarchy of the court in *The Trial*; the obscure bureaucracy of Count West-west in *The Castle*: all these explore different aspects of a fundamental problem. It would be a reductive use of Freud – whether or not Freud himself was so reductive I leave an open question – to suggest that all these examples were simply 'sublimations' of a basic psychological problem. The point might be better expressed by saying that the relationship with the father was simply the local condition upon which the imagination of the artist worked, discovering through it and beyond it areas of universal spiritual significance. To put it another way: the popularized-Freudian notion of God as a simple 'father-substitute' is a facile reading of a complicated relation. If man is a spiritual being, it is just as possible that relations between son and father are conditioned by the religious instinct, as that an idea of God is dependent on the human relationship.

Kafka's attitude to his father can be seen most clearly in the 'Letter to his Father' (a letter never sent). We see there a desperate attempt to work out the problem of their relationship. Kafka's attitude is a mixture of the finest love and admiration and violent criticism. The young Kafka adored his father's physique and vitality, his robust worldly strength of mind. Equally he detested his boorish manners, his self-pity, his unthinking cruelty to his children and his religious hypocrisy. He was a figure of overwhelming power to the young

111

Kafka, and seemed to hold in his hands the power of life and death. One incident in particular is related by Kafka: how his father once came into his bedroom when he was very small, and because he would not stop crying for water took him out on to the balcony that ran round the inner courtyard of the house and left him there. 'Even years afterwards I suffered from the tormenting fancy that the huge man, my father, the ultimate authority, would come almost for no reason at all and take me out of bed in the night and carry me out on to the *pavlatche*, and that therefore I was such a mere nothing for him' (p. 162). Kafka writes of how the most trivial occurrences, like his father's criticism of his table-manners when his father himself ate boorishly, affected his view of him profoundly, for

the man who was so tremendously the measure of all things for me, yourself did not keep the commandments imposed on me. Hence the world for me was divided into three parts: one in which I, the slave, lived under laws that had been invented only for me and which I could, I did not know why, never completely comply with; then a second world, which was infinitely remote from mine, in which you lived, concerned with government, with the issuing of orders and with annoyance about their not being obeyed; and finally a third world where everybody else lived happily and free from orders and from having to obey. (pp. 167–8)

There, in embryo, we have the worlds of *The Trial* and *The Castle*.

Kafka's lifelong preoccupation with the mysterious irrationality of authority did not *spring from* these early experiences: that would be a limitedly deterministic view. It sprung rather from his uniquely gifted nature, and that in itself is a mystery. It was this nature that caused him to react so profoundly and acutely to circumstances of this early relationship not in themselves so uncommon; and to see into the problem so deeply that it escaped in his work its limited psychological and familial confinement. As with his attitude towards his father, but in the haunting and disconcerting symbols of his art reaching far beyond that predicament, Kafka's attitude towards the authorities of his stories is compounded of attraction and repulsion, the outrage of the 'reasonable' man and the sense of inescapable duty of the religious man, the reaction, 'But this is absurd!', and the comic realization that truth lies somewhere in that absurdity, the sense of despair at the corruptness of the very 'authorities' to whom he is driven in search of judgement or justification, and the

Franz Kafka

odd turns of perspective that suddenly show them in a quite different light.

C. S. Lewis said that *Hamlet* was essentially the story of a man who has been given a task by a ghost:[7] I would like to amend that slightly and say that *Hamlet* is essentially the story of a man who has been given a task by *his father's* ghost. That it is a ghost, and that it is the ghost of his father, are distinct elements, equally important. Recent studies of the play have focused rightly and suggestively on the nature of the Ghost; but they have tended to ignore the other element: Hamlet's memory of his father as distinct from his response to the Ghost. How does Hamlet remember his father?

> So excellent a king, that was to this
> Hyperion to a satyr, so loving to my mother
> That he might not beteem the winds of heaven
> Visit her face too roughly. (I.ii. 139–42)

(This is his first soliloquy.) The epithet is godlike, and 'beteem the winds of heaven' also suggests a godlike power. Claudius on the contrary is cast in the role of a type of lechery: it is from the first his sensuality that Hamlet seizes on. In III.iv, the interview with the Queen, it is again a godlike quality in old Hamlet that Hamlet lauds in his description:

> See what a grace was seated on this brow:
> Hyperion's curls, the front of Jove himself,
> An eye like Mars, to threaten and command,
> A station like the herald Mercury
> Alighted on a heaven-kissing hill –
> A combination and a form indeed
> Where every god did seem to set his seal
> To give the world assurance of a man. (ll. 56–63)

Though at the end of the speech his emphasis is on the human, there is an idea here of the godlike *in* the human, the godlike attributes making 'a man' what he is. The same preoccupation is there in Hamlet's famous speech to Rosencrantz and Guildenstern:

What a piece of work is man, how noble in reason, how infinite in faculties, in form and moving how express and admirable, in action how like an angel, in apprehension how like a god. (II.ii. 312–19)

113

It also illustrates the strongly pagan element in Hamlet's imagination which coexists alongside the Christian elements. (We may remember here Lawrence's contrast between the old assertive pagan and aristocratic ego, and the new Christian and democratic consciousness. Hamlet remembers his father as 'a man' because he was like a god.)

What I am suggesting is that Hamlet goes a long way towards associating his father with the gods. And we may also note that Hamlet's references to the Christian God all see him in his role as giver of laws or as an overseeing providence: the 'Everlasting' who has 'fixed his canon 'gainst self-slaughter' or the 'divinity that shapes our ends', the 'special providence'. He never refers to Christ or the God of forgiveness. Hamlet's God is God the Father not God the Son. This association of his father with the gods helps to account for the strongly compelling nature that Hamlet feels in the Ghost's command. It is filial *piety* in a very strict sense. From the first he mistrusts the Ghost (as, we learn from Eleanor Prosser,[8] an Elizabethan just as much as ourselves would be prone to do), but there is simultaneously a sense of possibly divine mission:

> O all you host of heaven! O earth! What else?
> And shall I couple hell? (I.V. 92–3)

Later on he speaks of himself as 'prompted to my revenge by heaven and hell'. The possible association of the ghost of his father with *both* places is, in effect, the root of his dilemma. His memory of his father is of a godlike man who seems to him to sum up what a man is. His experience of the Ghost is of a shadowy and tormented figure suffering the fires of purgatory for his sins, dwelling with anguish on the horrible details of his murder, tormented with the thought of his wife's lust, and calling for revenge. The result is that Hamlet's idea of 'man' and of the 'divine' is radically divided between a noble memory and a horrifying apparition. We do not have to say with Ernest Jones that Hamlet 'really' hated his father and covered this up by an over-intense and idealizing admiration. The admiration is genuine. But in the Ghost Hamlet sees another side of his father which leads to a deep division in his mind, which remains inarticulate. It leads to a doubt about the very bases of life itself and what it is to be 'a man'. Hamlet's prophetic soul has a premonition of this

Franz Kafka

in his curious train of thought in the dialogue with Horatio after
his first soliloquy:

> The funeral baked meats
> Did coldly furnish forth the marriage tables.
> Would I had met my dearest foe in heaven
> Or ever I had seen that day, Horatio!
> My father, methinks I see my father.
> – Where, my lord?
> –   In my minds eye, Horatio.
> – I saw him once. 'A was a goodly king.
> – 'A was a man, take him for all in all,
>   I shall not look upon his like again.   (i.ii. 180–8)

'My dearest foe in heaven...my father' – the collocation is an
extraordinary one.[9] 'Dearest foe' almost sums up the Freudian
paradox, and 'in heaven' suggests the larger dimensions I have been
pointing to. What it suggests overall is a foretaste of the radical
confusion of perception of good and evil, heaven and hell, that is
Hamlet's dilemma (and a universal dilemma). The sense of the divine
comes to us through the agency of human perception, but that
agency is flawed because it is human. Kafka found in his father a
figure who was at the root of his idea of what it was to be a man:
but at the same time he found in him a boor, a hypocrite, and an
irrational tyrant. His father gave him his first experience of authority
but that authority was inexplicable, irrational, tyrannical and often
absurd. Hamlet derived from his father that sense of the godlike in
man that inspires 'What a piece of work is man': but in the Ghost
he finds an ambiguous and unregenerate figure burning in the
flames of jealousy.

As with Kafka, there is a close relation in *Hamlet* between the
ambiguous sense of the father and the sexual disgust. There is no
need to document Hamlet's manifestation of the latter yet again:
it is there from his very first soliloquy, through the nunnery-scene
with Ophelia, and becomes most violent in his scene with his mother
in Act III. The first soliloquy comes, of course, *before* he has seen
the Ghost. (Just as Kafka's sexual distaste and self-doubt did not
depend on his father's remarks to him at the ages of sixteen and
thirty-six.) But can we doubt that the Ghost's narrative intensified
this disgust? If the reader says 'Yes, we can' to that, I can merely

115

refer him to my fuller exploration of those scenes in my reading of the play in Part 2 of this study. I had better just ask him at this point only to entertain the possibility that the Ghost in i.v is not an unexceptionable authority conferring a 'sacred duty', and that his expression of disgust at the queen's infidelity is made as much in anger as in sorrow.

> But virtue, as it never will be moved,
> Through lewdness court it in the shape of heaven,
> So lust, though to a radiant angel linked,
> Will sate itself in a celestial bed
> And prey on garbage. (ll. 53–7)

Are those the accents of the impersonal messenger of justice who might be a fit figure to confer a 'sacred duty', or rather the tormented tones of a suffering jealousy? We have, at least, no *other* evidence that Gertrude's love of Claudius was so exclusively and degenerately lustful. What the Ghost is imputing to Gertrude is similar to what Kafka's father was imputing to him in his conversations about sex: that he was somehow outside the pale of a healthy love or a noble sexuality. Of course the cases are different, and old Hamlet has some provocation for his view! But there is the similarity in the paternal disillusion which in effect does help to 'taint' Hamlet's mind, though the Ghost warns him against the possibility. Because of the way we experience the time-sequence while reading through or watching the play, we feel from Ophelia's report that Hamlet must have gone straight from the battlements to her closet and to have fallen to that perusal of her face that so frightened her. And it is because of what the Ghost says that Hamlet becomes so preoccupied with his mother's guilt and so involved with that preoccupation in Act III. There is then, a corrupt side to the Ghost, which conjoins with his awesome authority as a revenant from the grave and with the idealized, godlike memory that Hamlet has of his father. It is this conjunction – one might say, of 'heaven and hell' – that is the source of Hamlet's inability to carry out his revenge.

There is, further, one other aspect of Hamlet's attitude to his father that seems worth noting, and that is his emphasis on his father's physical beauty. In the description quoted above it is this that strikes one: 'Hyperion's curls, the front of Jove himself / An

116

eye like Mars', etc. It is the 'combination and a form' that gives the world assurance of a man. How could Gertrude have given herself to a man so *physically* different from her husband:

> Have you eyes?
> Could you on this fair mountain leave to feed,
> And batten on this moor? Ha! Have you eyes? (iii.iv. 68–70)

And later,

> Eyes without feeling, feeling without sight,
> Ears without hands or eyes, smelling sans all,
> Or but a sickly part of one true sense
> Could not so mope. (ll. 79–82)

It is the bewitchment of her physical senses, not of her moral sense, at which Hamlet is amazed (though granted we may see the two as related). Like Kafka, again, Hamlet is impressed by his father's beauty, his physique, his physical manliness. 'He was a man, take him for all in all.'

If this is accepted, it may throw some light on the significance of the Ghost's speech in i.v. We may remember how the Ghost, too, is appalled by Gertrude's seduction by a man so physically inferior,

> a wretch whose natural gifts were poor
> To those of mine. (ll. 51–2)

And also how obsessively the Ghost dwells on the physical effects of the poison on his body.

> And in the porches of my ear did pour
> The leperous distilment, whose effect
> Holds such an enmity with the blood of man
> That swift as quicksilver it courses through
> The natural gates and alleys of the body,
> And with a sudden vigour it doth posset
> And curd, like eager droppings into milk,
> The thin and wholesome blood. So did it mine,
> And a most instant tetter barked about
> Most lazarlike with vile and loathsome crust
> All my smooth body. (ll. 63–73)

It is, incidentally, a masterly example of Shakespeare's most vital and particular verse, and it conveys a sharpness of physical disgust that cannot but make an impression on us. The Ghost is obsessed, one might almost say morally tainted, by what the poison did to his body. It is so much the central feature of his narration that we must assume it has a significance. Can we not say that it is a morbid and almost narcissistic dwelling on the physical details? And that it is a part of what makes the Ghost into a suspicious kind of messenger?[10] And when we put this together with the kind of admiration that Hamlet has for his father that I have just noted we see a possible connection. In speaking of his murder in just this way the Ghost is likely to act on Hamlet's feelings particularly powerfully. He learns not merely of his father's murder, but hears this account of how his body, the physical beauty of which Hamlet so admired, was tainted and corrupted.

These things add up to a peculiar impression which is difficult to interpret. But it seems to involve a peculiarly intense relation between father and son, a relation in which the father's physical beauty and virility are the focus of the son's passionate admiration, and the corruption of that beauty the focus of the horror of his death. Might one tentatively suggest (without going into the deeper waters of psychology) that there is here a passionate sense of male beauty which is a part of Hamlet's particular kind of idealism? Certainly he has little or nothing to say about female beauty: talking to Ophelia he is entirely disillusioned with it: 'I have heard of your paintings well enough.' And even in his letter to Ophelia in an earlier and happier period (one assumes), he is entirely without conviction and eloquence in his praise of her: 'beautified' *is* a vile phrase.

May I hasten to reassure the reader that I am not about to propose a 'homosexual' Hamlet (no doubt he has been proposed before). But who would now deny that the sexual problem is central to the play? And it also seems that one can say that Hamlet's noble idealism does have as its concomitant a disgust for the flesh, not just in the first soliloquy, but at moments throughout the play. Hamlet's sense of man is godlike, 'in action how like an angel, in apprehension how like a god'. And it is the human form, above all, that in his descriptions of his father he emphasizes as godlike. When the Ghost dwells on the corruption of his body by the poison he strikes at the roots of Hamlet's feelings. We might even feel that the imagery of hidden disease which reappears in Hamlet's later speeches derives partly from the impact of this description of actual disease. It has also been pointed out that the poisoning in the ear has sexual symbolic overtones; and the Serpent is often portrayed whispering into the ear of Eve. It has been said too that the effects the Ghost describes are like the effects of syphilis (which entered England in the sixteenth century).[11] The cumulative impression is of a sexual contamination, even of a contamination *by* sex. In narrating the account of his death so powerfully and obsessively the Ghost *does* help to taint Hamlet's mind, to intensify the sexual disgust of his first soliloquy, to throw him into the toils of disillusion with Ophelia, and to fill his mind with the images of 'rank corruption' which erupt in the interview with the queen. The godlike father has been corrupted by a sexual poison – and the knowledge of it taints the son's mind. Hamlet surely has grounds for saying, 'The spirit I have seen may be the devil.'

The general question of the flawed nature of human perception is a fundamental theme in *Hamlet* as it is a recurring subject for Kafka. How should we 'see' Hamlet? At his own valuation? From a romantic position which enjoins a fundamental sympathy and identification with the hero? How should we see Claudius? Hamlet tells us that he is a lecher, and physically repulsive (a 'mildewed ear'), but we *see* none of these things and receive no corroboration of them: indeed what we do see of Claudius suggests a quite different figure. What is the matter with Hamlet (ask the King and Queen)? 'There's matter in these sighs.' In no other play is the question What is going on? so often asked in some form by the characters in the play: and no other play has been questioned so often by its readers in the same words. Can Hamlet be sure of the Ghost, or be sure that he has seen the Ghost aright? His imaginations may be 'as foul as Vulcan's stithy'.

The problem of perceiving good and evil is one with which Kafka was continually preoccupied, perhaps more subtly and profoundly than any other writer of this century. His aphorisms express in compressed form what his novels explore. 'Evil knows of the Good, but Good does not know of Evil.' 'Evil is a radiation of the human consciousness in certain transitional positions. It is not actually the sensual world which is a mere appearance, what is so is the evil of it, which, admittedly, is what constitutes the sensual world in our eyes.'[12] Evil for Kafka is a product of our perceptions. Only the good is real. How then can Hamlet distinguish between what his way of seeing creates for him and what is really there? Is the love between Claudius and Gertrude simply a gross matter of lust (as Hamlet sees it); or are we to attach weight to the King's seemingly genuine and deep feeling later in the play?

This difficulty of perceiving leads to a kind of comedy, what one might call the comedy of the distorting mirror. The mirror is the perception. It is an element in Hamlet's fooling with Polonius:

– Do you see yonder cloud that's almost in the shape of a camel?
– By th' mass and 'tis, like a camel indeed.
– Methings it is like a weasel.
– It is backed like a weasel.
– Or like a whale.
– Very like a whale. (III.ii. 385–90)

(It might be the dialogue on the subject of *Hamlet*. If Shakespeare had been given to cryptic subtitles in the manner of modern books of criticism he might have subtitled *Hamlet*, 'Very Like a Whale'.) It is also there in the cellarage episode, in Hamlet's strange foolery with the Ghost. In sudden, nearly hysterical relief of his feelings he turns the Ghost into a comic demon: 'Well said, old mole, canst work in the earth so fast? A worthy pioner', and 'Ha, ha, boy, say'st thou so. Art thou there truepenny. Come on. You hear this fellow in the cellarage.' As a relief for his feelings Hamlet is making the Ghost into something comic. Compare this to Kafka's story 'The Judgement', where the hero sees his father as a childish buffoon, as an unconscious way of protecting himself from his authority. And of course the father *is* comic as well as terrifying. This is what gives the story its uncanny power: that it recognizes the reality of the father's authority while simultaneously seeing its absurdity. The father is a means of understanding the nature of God: at the same time of course he is only a human father. To a mind like Kafka's this paradox was at the root of his beliefs and his confusions.

'He has pockets even in his shirt!' said Georg to himself, and believed that with this remark he could make him an impossible figure for all the world. Only for a moment did he think so, since he kept on forgetting everything.[13]

'The Judgement' is the tragicomic story of how this confusion destroys the hero. By writing it Kafka escaped being destroyed himself, or rather he *did* destroy himself symbolically, in the imagination, so that he could die to his old self and move on to further creation, becoming more what he really was. The hero's perception of his father in 'The Judgement' is divided between two irreconcilable extremes, both of which distort. Can we not see Hamlet's perception of the Ghost, as both a grand messenger of justice and an 'old mole', as similarly divided?

There are other elements of *Hamlet* which reinforce, I think, the suggestion that we can get nearer to the meaning of the play by seeing it in the light of the Kafkaesque. Rosencrantz and Guildenstern remind me of Kafka's 'pairs' of characters: the two executioners in *The Trial*, Delmarche and Robinson in *America*, and most of all the two assistants in *The Castle*, who sometimes seem genuinely to be helping K. and at others merely hindering him. Again, Osric, who comes to lead Hamlet to his death, is the most ridiculous figure in *Hamlet*: and in *The Trial* the two executioners who lead Joseph K. to his death are more laughable than any of the officials connected with the court. The agencies behind the death of both heroes are at their most absurd as the fate of each nears its culmination. And like Joseph K., Hamlet cooperates in his own death and meets it with a kind of acceptance. (Are Rosencrantz and Guildenstern good friends to Hamlet or not? The question is not so simply answered either, for presumably they are as perplexed as anyone about Hamlet's mad behaviour and, not only out of obedience to the king but also as friends concerned with his welfare, they try to find out what is the matter with him. Nothing in the text contradicts this view.) Polonius also reminds me of Joseph K.'s uncle in *The Trial*, with his blustering incomprehension and confidence that he can solve the problem of Joseph's arrest.

Finally, here is a meditation of Kafka's on the subject of self-knowledge.

'Know thyself' does not mean 'Observe thyself'. 'Observe thyself' is what the Serpent says. It means: 'Make yourself master of your actions.' But you are so already, you are the master of your actions. So that saying means: 'Misjudge yourself! Destroy yourself!' which is something evil – and only if one bends down very far indeed does one also hear the good in it, which is 'In order to make of yourself what you are'.[14]

No other Shakespearian tragic hero *watches himself* as much as

Hamlet, not even Macbeth. Perhaps only Iago watches himself as much, but without moral judgement or control. Hamlet tries to make himself master of his actions, and in the end does indeed 'destroy himself', or, at the least, lets himself be destroyed. For the first part of the play he observes himself in a way that does have an element of the serpent in it. But after his return from the voyage to England he seems to let things go. Does he in the end 'make of himself what he is'? Does he *become* anything? Critics have spent centuries bending very far down indeed to discover what Hamlet becomes, what he makes of himself. Perhaps only the fact that the play and the hero have endured so strongly for such a length of time suggests that there is something *there*, that Hamlet becomes something significant. It seems to me however that we are left at the end of the play with a number of different perspectives and that there is no final lasting impression that Hamlet has proved a tragic *hero*. Mallarmé spoke of the latent man of nobility which Hamlet could never become. It is not that there is no real image behind the distorting mirrors; Hamlet does not despair of the problem of finding it so much as relinquishes the task. His tragedy, as I have suggested before, is one of ignorance; of the fact that he does *not* 'make of himself what he is'.

9

Hamlet and modern literature

Identity, self-knowledge, and perception

What over-all impression can be formed of *Hamlet* from the tradition, as I think it can be called, of the creative use of the play as a source of allusion, myth, mask and symbol? Despite the differences of the writers discussed, the differences of genre and the fact that they see *Hamlet* in different ways, certain common preoccupations do emerge, elements which it seems to me must be present in any modern reading of the play.

The first of these might be described as a preoccupation with Hamlet's 'identity', with what finally, if anything does, constitutes the essence of his character. And this preoccupation seems to be inevitably involved in the modern period with the idea of the ambiguity of Hamlet's experience. All the writers I have been discussing see Hamlet's 'character' as uncertain, shifting, impossible to speak of in any single and simple way. After contemplating the Hamlet of these writers it would seem that no view which ignores either the 'sweet prince' or the 'arrant knave' can claim to account fully for the play; so that neither the romantic view of Coleridge, and of Bradley after him, nor the opposing modern view of, say, Wilson Knight, can seem adequate on its own. There is in the creative 'interpretations' which I have discussed a common theme of doubt about the good and evil in Hamlet, a need to give due weight to both sides. In Mallarmé, Hamlet is a type of the hero of the spirit who seeks, like the symbolist poet, to create or act in such a way as to embody the truth of life in his creation or action, to banish chance from a conception of life and discover a sense of freedom and order. But he is also the 'mauvais Hamlet' who may destroy himself and the lives around him in the effort towards this ideal, the 'black doubter' whose hesitation spreads poison. His nobility

123

remains only latent, a 'jewel intact beneath the disaster', but it is never *realized*. In *Igitur* the hero seems to separate his finite, limited self from his true self, which watches the former disappearing into the mirror. There seems here to be a kind of crystallization of identity. But the upshot is curious: having become himself, the only task for the young prince is to die. There is no vengeance to perform as in *Hamlet*. The work seems as I have said to be a kind of private ritual to free Mallarmé from 'the monster of impotence' – Igitur dies and Mallarmé is left to create. The *personnage* referred to in *Igitur* seems, I have suggested, to be the hero's 'character', that romantic conception of identity which dominated nineteenth-century Shakespeare criticism and which is here described as an anachronism. Igitur's *personnage*, his romantic 'identity', is what disappears into the mirror: Mallarmé frees himself from the 'self'. In his criticism of *Hamlet* Mallarmé sees the hero's nature as radically ambiguous: in his own creations inspired by *Hamlet* and drawing on play and hero he seeks to explore this ambiguous identity and separate out its elements, so that the pure creative principle can emerge. In 'Le Pitre Châtié' the clown tries to shed his role but finds he needs its protective covering. In *Igitur* the hero separates his essential self from the inessential. In 'Un Coup de Dés' the young hero, dimly glimpsed, is utterly destroyed in the storm, but the dice is thrown and the constellation, the poem, remains: here 'identity' and self are abandoned utterly to leave the pure detached utterance.

Does Hamlet achieve any firm sense of self or identity, or does he too abandon it, and act not decisively (that is, with resolution), but abandon himself to chance? What *is* Hamlet at the end of the play – a noble hero who deserves a soldier's burial? A man who has made a mess of things? As I have argued elsewhere, the feeling that chance is dominant and that Hamlet acts merely because he is prompted by events seems to me the strongest one; and we are left with various different views of Hamlet, none of which finally sums him up. And yet Claudius has been killed: perhaps we can say that as in 'Un Coup de Dés' the fall of the hero has, for him, 'no human result' – it does not crystallize or fix his identity in any way – but through it the action is carried out.

Claudel, like Laforgue, seems to respond particularly to the 'antic' side of Hamlet when, in a letter to Marcel Schwob, he remarks that 'after the apparition of the inhabitant of the other world [Hamlet] does no more on this side of the stage of life than to play a role'.[1] One might expand this by saying that once Hamlet has glimpsed beyond the grave some kind of ultimate spiritual state, however ambiguous, his life and actions on earth seem, *sub specie aeternitatis*, to lose reality and to become a passing show. Claudel also, like Mallarmé, seems in this letter to see Hamlet as unable to impinge decisively on events while alive, and able only by his death to bring anything about: 'Minister of death, it is only when dead already himself that [Hamlet] will be able to carry out death's works' (pp. 1455–6) – and the phrases here have overtones of destructiveness which relate Claudel's view to Wilson Knight's essay 'The Embassy of Death'.

Valéry does not directly consider Hamlet's 'identity', but one of his remarks about the difference between a finished work of literature and its author's intention bears on the question. 'Once the work has appeared its interpretation by the author has no more validity than anyone else's interpretation.'[2] And his comment on this a few lines later suggests how *Hamlet* is a particularly apt example of a work, and a character, who leave themselves open to many interpretations and even to recreations like the examples considered in the present study: 'Once [the work of art] has appeared, others use it as they wish – cf. Hamlet, Tartuffe' (p. 1191). It is particularly Hamlet's lack of 'identity', I would suggest, that makes him so fitting an example in this case.

Laforgue uses the mask of Hamlet to embody his sense of himself as the failed idealist or idealist-turned-decadent, at once expressing and mocking his disgust at life. In this way he questions the violence of any attempt on his part at heroism, and shows himself unworthy to be a hero, but preserves the echo of that sense of life in his new awareness. In his ironic version of the Hamlet story, and in the poems of Laforgue's middle period, the first part of this process is evident. But at the same time there is, in his use of epigraphs from the nunnery-scene, a tendency to stress Hamlet's and his own cynicism and satiric bitterness. In Laforgue we see brought to life the element of the fool or 'antic' in Hamlet's character, the buffoonery and self-mockery by which Hamlet seems to evade any decisive action and self-definition, the self-mockery of 'your only

125

jig-maker', who makes up little rhymes and jests to lighten the burden of those crucial moments in the play like the one after the Play-scene, where Hamlet talks of getting 'a fellowship with a cry of players'. Laforgue intensifies our sense of Hamlet as the Fool, that element which Gilbert Murray pointed out was from the first a feature of the Hamlet myth (Amloði in Saxo's version meaning 'the fool'). In the *Derniers Vers* the satirical element is less self-righteous and there is a new kind of decency and generosity – particularly towards his Ophelias – without suggesting any self-congratulation at the achievement. He begins to incorporate into his poetic self those elements of generosity that we see in Hamlet (towards Horatio, or the Players). Laforgue sees himself still as confused and indeterminate, but with a newly clarified sense of what that confusion is like, a new sense of proportion. And I suggest that this is remarkably like Shakespeare's Hamlet, who returns from England not resolved, but with a calmer sense of his own confusion.

T. S. Eliot, using Hamlet ironically in juxtaposition with Prufrock, reminds us both of the traditional heroic Hamlet and at the same time of Hamlet the Fool: the contrast modifies both characters. In his essay 'Hamlet and his Problems' he points to Hamlet's obsessiveness, his possession by something he cannot express. In 'Little Gidding' we see the poet in the process of achieving a new self-awareness, almost creating a new identity, 'knowing myself yet being someone other', at the moment when he meets *his* ghost. Eliot is moving beyond the spirit of harhness, the mood of 'things ill done and done to others' harm / Which once you took for exercise of virtue'. *Four Quartets* is partly the creation of a new, profounder poetic identity. It shows by contrast something of the spirit that Shakespeare's Hamlet lacks, the spirit of remorse for things ill done, of forgiveness, and the need for the 'refining fire'. Hamlet never achieves this kind of profound identity, which sheds the Prufrockian foolery and the moralist's self-righteousness. Torn between his command to put an end to an evil usurper and his sense of the confusion of his own spirit he can only finally act in a spirit of fatalism and egoism (as I shall try to illustrate in Part 2).

Joyce's *Ulysses* has for one of its main subjects the discovery of a new artistic identity via the development of Stephen. At the end of *A Portrait of the Artist* Stephen is a kind of self-righteous Hamlet, and this persists in much of *Ulysses*. He is out to rid Ireland of 'the Priest and the King', but he is also aware of the confusion in himself, the priggishness, melancholy, and lack of humanity. His theory of *Hamlet* is the product of a deep sense of doubt about life and creativity, and he sees the play as the product of the spirit of jealousy and revenge. In the psychological melting-pot of the 'Circe' episode this kind of consciousness begins to be dissolved and the theory of *Hamlet* is evaporated by exaggeration. And in the meeting with Bloom we see a new Stephen beginning to develop, a self modified by the awareness of Bloom, a movement towards the ideal artistic view of life, the 'sane and joyful spirit'. Does Hamlet move in this direction by the end of the play? We need only recall the morbid reflections of the graveyard scene, or that as he goes off to the duel all is ill about his heart. Hamlet never achieves a fully human sense of the world. But Joyce's presentation of *Hamlet* as it exists in the mind of Bloom reminds us that the play is not all Hamlet the character. The spirit of the gravediggers makes us aware of a simpler and more robust sense of life which, together with other suggestions in the play, give us a context in which to view the dilemma of Hamlet himself.

In Lawrence the question of Hamlet's 'identity', that which constitutes his true being, is central. He makes us aware of the conflict between Hamlet's sincerity and his obsessions. He sees Hamlet as the type of the Renaissance European who becomes disillusioned with the flesh, the 'ego', the idea of aristocracy and the king. His Hamlet is a Puritan and a regicide. He cannot 'be' in the body, in the old assertion of the ego, yet he is commanded to 'be' by avenging his father. He hovers between this vengeful assertion and the resignation, the 'not-being' of Christian spirituality. There is, for Lawrence, no reconciliation between the two at the end. Hamlet does not achieve an identity: one might say that this is Hamlet's fundamental tragic failure.

In the Kierkegaardian view of *Hamlet* the same sense of conflicting possibilities of good and evil is also central. Hamlet can never be either the hero or just the neurotic meddler (a Gregers Werle) because he is made up of too many elements which never resolve themselves into an identity. The action of the play is the postponing of the moment of decisive action which would crystallize this identity, or rather a magnification of that period before action in order to consider it fully. Hamlet is 'shut up', never reveals himself fully. The conflict between his demoniacal nature and his heroic and humane nature is never settled, and I think Kierkegaard would have seen this as the essence of the tragedy. In all the other Shakesperian tragedies the protagonist *does* reveal himself, takes the step into the tragic action which decides his fate, and reveals the depth of his nature in which the good is defeated by the evil but not destroyed. All the other tragic heroes are forced at some point to face what they have done and to know themselves, although in Lear the realization that 'I am a very foolish fond old man' is fleeting, and in Othello a self-deception, a clinging to heroism, persists to the end. But in *Hamlet* all is confusion, and Hamlet can only say 'I do not know': his 'real self' is still at the end in a kind of latent state (Mallarmé spoke of the 'latent hero' in Hamlet). Hamlet has, in this sense, not been 'put on', as Fortinbras says. 'Courtier, soldier, scholar', 'sweet prince', 'arrant knave' – Hamlet has become none of these: they are still all in solution at the end of the play.

Hamlet, this train of thought suggests, is a tragedy of identity. I mean the phrase to incorporate the idea of self-knowledge, and the perception of others' identities. For without the latter there can be no achievement of identity, the sense of a known self and its relations with others. Kierkegaard's 'dread' is a dread of what the self may become, or rather what it will turn out to be when revealed. It is, as I suggested above, an ignorance of the self and the future. Claudel suggested a Hamlet (and a Mallarmé) who was a 'professeur d'attention', attentive to the signs which surround him, each of which carries a hidden meaning. The world of *Hamlet*, for all the characters in the play, is a world of such signs, and they remain enigmatic. None of the characters, in answer to their question, What may this mean?, ever discovers fully what is going on and how much the others know. Claudius dies without revealing whether he realizes that Hamlet knows about the exact circumstances of his crime. Nor does his guilt ever 'unkennel itself in one speech' as Hamlet hoped it would. We do not know exactly how much Hamlet tells Horatio, or how much Horatio credits it. We do not know exactly how much Hamlet loved Ophelia, or why Ophelia calls Hamlet 'unkind' so early in the nunnery scene – before his unkindness has shown itself in the play.[3] Rosencrantz and Guildenstern do not pluck out the heart of Hamlet's mystery, but nor does anyone else, and nor does the play. 'Do you see yonder cloud that's almost in the shape of a camel?', Hamlet asks Polonius. And Polonius:

– By th' mass and 'tis, like a camel indeed.
– Methinks it is like a weasel.
– It is backed like a weasel.
– Or like a whale.
– Very like a whale.

Shapes are ambiguous and uncertain in *Hamlet*, perception is blurred. Did the King see the Dumb Show? If so, what did he see? Does Hamlet interpret his reaction correctly? We do not know. Our perception is mainly through the eyes of Hamlet, but we cannot be sure that those eyes themselves are clear because we cannot know Hamlet himself. If, in Kafka's words, 'Evil is a radiation of the human consciousness in certain transitional positions' (see above, p. 119), we must say that Hamlet's consciousness seems to remain in some transitional position, so that we cannot be sure if Hamlet has seen evil and detached it from himself, or if he is still involved in it and projecting it on what he sees.

– Who's there?
– Nay, answer me. Stand and unfold yourself.

But Hamlet's self is never unfolded.

Authority

The questions of identity, self-knowledge and perception which are raised in the modern creative use of *Hamlet* are closely involved with the question of authority. And this seems to me to take an equal place, both in the play itself and in the imaginative creations of the modern writers I have discussed. It takes an equal place in the play because it is with the problem of the Ghost that the play begins: What is the nature of this being who gives the commandment to Hamlet which is his great burden? Does it in any way confer a 'sacred duty'? Is it a spiritual authority? Hamlet says in Act IV:

I do not know
Why yet I live to say 'This thing's to do',

Modern writers and the ghosts of *Hamlet*

> Sith I have cause, and will, and strength, and means
> To do't.   (IV.iv. 43–6)

Cause and will and strength and means: but what is lacking here is the idea of 'justification'. 'Cause', I take it, is simply used in the sense of 'motive'. What Hamlet lacks is an ultimate sense of authorization, that 'intuition of the soul' which Lawrence says is the only source of true justice. The preoccupation with this in the *Hamlet* of the modern writers may be briefly recapitulated.

In Mallarmé's *Igitur* the hero has to detach himself from his initial awareness of the presence of his ancestors, of 'un age supérieur', in order to act with creative originality and further the life of his race rather than just repeat it. He has to close the book of magic and the volume of science and act on his own creative impulse. In 'Un Coup de Dés' an ancient mariner or hero haunts the scene of the shipwreck, but it is the younger hero who throws the dice. In Laforgue's *Moralité* the 'irregular decease' of old Hamlet is referred to ironically. There is no ghost, but there is the suspicion that Hamlet's whole idea of his father's murder may be just a figment of his diseased imagination – an imagination bloodier and wilder even than that of Shakespeare's Hamlet in his most tormented moments.

Claudel, as we have seen, touches on the question of the authority of the Ghost when he says that after this glimpse from another world Hamlet loses his sense of the reality of this world. But one might add that this is no specifically Christian apprehension of the vanity of earthly things, since the ghostly authority he has seen is an ambiguous one: Hamlet is left not with a sense of an ultimate Christian duty, but for much of the time merely a sense, as Claudel says, that he is playing a role. Valéry, as we saw briefly in Chapter 2, also touches on the significance of the Ghost as an authority when he uses Hamlet and the Ghost as images of modern European man and his relation to tradition.

In Eliot the ghost of 'Little Gidding' is a kind of counter-ghost to that in *Hamlet*. The combined presence of all Eliot's 'dead masters' is here conjured in order to learn from it the limitations of that idealism and humanism which they have bequeathed to Eliot, that idealism which led, perhaps, to 'things ill done and done to others' harm / Which once you took for exercise of virtue'. The character

130

of this ghost is profoundly beneficent rather than ambiguous. It warns the poet of what to expect in old age, 'the cold friction of expiring sense', 'the laceration of laugher at what ceases to amuse' – the kind of laughter which Hamlet is already experiencing in the graveyard scene, as he jests bitterly on how a king may go a progress through the guts of a beggar. 'Then fools' approval stings, and honour stains': Hamlet too has been stung by the useless, well-meaning friendship of Rosencrantz and Guildenstern. And his honour is deeply stained by the deaths of the two courtiers, and the deaths of Polonius and Ophelia, and by his 'taking refuge in dishonesty' (as Johnson put it) in his excuses to Laertes: and all this before he has had a chance to become old. All his wisdom, too, is 'useless in the darkness into which you look / Or from which you turn your eyes'. And the ghost in 'Little Gidding' points to an authority higher than himself, which Hamlet is never able to perceive:

> that refining fire
> Where you must move in measure, like a dancer. (ll. 145–6)

Eliot is conscious, in his poem 'Gerontion', of 'depraved May'. The Ghost in *Hamlet* thinks of his sins in a similar image: 'Cut off even in the blossoms of my sin'; and Hamlet remembers them in a crucial moment 'with all his crimes broad blown, as flush as May'. But Eliot manages in his later poetry to detach himself from this disabling consciousness and imagine another kind of fire than the fire of sin. Hamlet at the end of the play is still immersed in that consciousness:

> Here, thou incestuous, murderous, damnèd Dane,
> Drink off this potion. Is thy union here.
> Follow my mother.   (v.ii. 326–8)

Eliot in his essay on 'Hamlet and his Problems' alludes to Montaigne's *Apologie de Raimond Sebond* as being relevant to Shakespeare's state of mind when he wrote *Hamlet*. And the burden of that essay (as I shall suggest below) is that man is a fool to think of himself as godlike and that without faith his mind cannot 'be maintained'. But Hamlet thinks of his father as a Jove, a Mars, a Mercury. He cannot come to terms with the Ghost's command, follow it or reject it, because of the peculiar combination in the Ghost of supernatural authority and human failing. Unlike Igitur, or the poet in 'Little

Gidding', he cannot detach himself enough from it to achieve a genuine identity.

In Joyce the Ghost is at the centre of Stephen Dedalus's theory of the play. It associates itself in Joyce's language with all the ghosts of the past which Stephen must combat or obey. Stephen's theory is an oppression to him because it suggests that the Ghost is merely consumed with unregenerate torment and hatred, jealousy and vengefulness, and that the Ghost is essentially Shakespeare. In encountering Bloom he encounters (one might say) a very different cuckolded husband – and one who represents other possibilities of tradition and other kinds of life. He becomes a kind of second father to Stephen and initiates him (and even more Joyce) into a sense of life which is unidealistic and unheroic, and yet conscientious, decent, and even touched by a life of thought and imagination. And the reader encounters in Bloom the way in which Shakespeare's play has its own life in an unliterary mind. It indirectly reminds the student of *Hamlet* that the play exists in popular tradition, not only as melodrama, but as thought and poetry. It also reminds him that the kind of consciousness which imagined the obsessive torments of Hamlet and the Ghost was free enough also to take delight in Hamlet's conversation with the Players, Claudius's love for Gertrude, and the comic robustness of the gravediggers. Stephen was in danger of thinking that Shakespeare in his most famous tragedy was motivated by hatred, and that he himself was trapped in a resentment of his own society which would always hamper free creation. We can, I think, see Hamlet's own problems springing directly from similar doubts about his Ghost. But unlike Stephen he never detaches himself from them, so that *Hamlet*, unlike *Ulysses*, is a tragedy.

D. H. Lawrence does not have much direct discussion of the Ghost, but in *Twilight in Italy* he says he finds it 'really one of the play's failures, it is so trivial and unspiritual and vulgar' (p. 82). The memorable thing about his reference to it is the comic story of his visit as a child to a travelling theatre, which for ever spoilt the Ghost for him:

The Ghost had on a helmet and a breastplate. I sat in pale transport.
  ''Amblet, 'Amblet, I am thy father's ghost.'

Then came a voice from the dark, silent audience, like a cynical knife
to my fond soul:
'Why tha arena, I can tell thy voice.'   (p. 82)

Lawrence is very much concerned with the question of the old
king's authority and power, and how Hamlet, he suggests, is torn
between assuming them in the old pagan and aristocratic way and
renouncing them in the Christian way. And Lawrence might indeed,
although he does not, have drawn some connection between what
he sees as the unspiritual nature of the Ghost, and Hamlet's doubt
of its authority and of whether or not to become 'the King and the
Father, in the self, supreme' (p. 77).

Kierkegaard does not mention the Ghost directly, but simply in
passing as the confirmation of Hamlet's dread. To probe what that
confirmation precisely is, I think we can say that it does not only
confirm Hamlet in his unarticulated suspicions of foul play, but also
in his dread of *himself*. Its narrative intensifies just those obsessive
qualities of Hamlet's mind which we have seen in the first soliloquy.
This is why Hamlet still thinks in ii.ii: 'The spirit I have seen / May
be a devil.' The possibility of the good or evil of the action before
which Hamlet hovers cannot be settled by reference to the Ghost,
who is himself ambiguous. It is interesting to note that Hegel (in
whom Kierkegaard was widely read) sees Hamlet's initial disbelief
in the Ghost as the profoundest trait in his character.[4] It makes his
consciousness purer than that of Oedipus or Orestes, says Hegel,
because these heroes simply follow the biddings of the sphinx or of
the gods. Hegel likens the priestess (through whom the gods speak)
to the witches in *Macbeth* who drive the hero to crime because he
believes in what they equivocally say. Hamlet is a purer consciousness because he tests the Ghost's story. But we can, I think, go
further, and say that even this testing does not settle the matter.
Hamlet remains in a state of dread before the possibility of good or
evil.

This dread is not articulated in terms of the good or evil of the
revenge in particular, which is why the ethical issue is scarcely raised
in the play. It is rather a pervasive doubt of the self and its ability
to perceive things aright (not just morally but in general). It is a
doubt of the grounds of action, of whatever it is in life that seems
to give men the authority to act, whether it be the sense of divine

injunction, the conviction of deep feeling, a belief in moral absolutes, a 'categorical imperative', or just the law of the jungle or instinctive self-preservation. And this doubt of the fundamental perception of authority is what gives one grounds for associating *Hamlet* with Kafka. Kafka's books are filled with 'ghosts' – ghostly authorities which the heroes seek in vain to reveal, test or challenge. But their final significance, like that of the Ghost in *Hamlet*, and like *Hamlet* itself, remains out of reach. A recent writer on Kafka describes his ability 'to foil us constantly in pursuit of meaning'[5] – while at the same time, one would add, giving us the conviction that we are drawn closer and closer to some revelation. *Hamlet* foils us constantly in pursuit of its meaning, and constantly provokes our interpretations.

Authority, or rather the perception of authority: it is not a key which unlocks the problem of *Hamlet*. But it does seem to be an aspect of the play which stands out among those aspects to which modern writers have most responded, together with the essential idea of Hamlet as a 'divided man', and the idea of the fallibilities of perception. If these things are there in the play they are the fitting discoveries of an age which has felt acutely the ambiguities of temporal and spiritual authority, the relativities of perception, and the problems of identity.

PART 2

Perception, authority, and identity:
a reading of *Hamlet*

Perception, authority, and identity:
a reading of *Hamlet*

The previous chapter attempted to identify certain common pre-occupations in different modern writers' responses to *Hamlet*. The reading of the play that follows attempts a fuller and more systematic account of how these preoccupations arise in the play and might be seen to govern our general sense of it. Whether or not I have manipulated the play to make it fit the ideas will, of course, be the crucial thing for the reader (if he has followed me this far) to decide. But in any event I hope I shall have revealed certain facets of the play, and ones which have striking affinities to many modern literary preoccupations. My rough sketch of the play would go something like this: Hamlet receives a command from a ghost; he has to understand the nature of that command if he can; he then has to act or refrain from action – this action or inaction will define him. We begin, then, with the problem of the Ghost's authority; then move to the problems of Hamlet's perception; and finally to the action and self-definition (if any) which follow.

But this is to see things largely from Hamlet's point of view, and there are other ways in which the play raises these three problems. It is full of secondary examples of dubious or ambiguous authority; it is also full of characters (other than Hamlet) who have to try and *interpret* events, to find out what is happening, to assure themselves of their perceptions, to make enquiries, and search or even spy out the truth. They are most of the time trying to find out about Hamlet, to assure themselves of what is the matter with him.

The three problems are questions also for the audience. The play deliberately gives us more than one perspective on the action. We too doubt the authority of the Ghost and the nature of Hamlet. We also doubt, in a larger sense, the 'authority' of the play as a whole, that is to say, what final view it is giving us. Reading or watching the play is an exercise in perception and in identification. If one had to give a label to the play it might be best to call it a tragedy of perception. But I would prefer not to tie myself to this description, and leave the three elements of the above title in play.

The following reading does not take the play scene by scene. This is in some ways a disadvantage, because in the end any persuasive reading must follow the linear experience of the play as we follow it on the page or in the theatre. But to do this would perhaps take too long, and would not highlight those things that I think need to be highlighted. Nevertheless, I have tried as much as possible to preserve a sense of dramatic context, and of course the arguments stand or fall by the sense they make when we return to the experience of the play itself. The following reading does take things roughly chronologically, however. It begins with an examination of the Ghost in the first act (section I); goes on to explore more fully our sense of Hamlet in the first two acts (II); and particularly with the Players (III); then examines the play-scene and how it affects our understanding of the Ghost and Hamlet (IV); and follows up Hamlet's subsequent behaviour and the second appearance of the Ghost (V). In section VI there is a discussion of other parts of the play which are not directly about Hamlet himself, and of what contribution these make to the main ideas of the play. Part VII looks at the end of the play and our final impressions; and VIII attempts a summing up.

I

'The Hamlet Formula', wrote C. S. Lewis, 'is not "a man who has to avenge his father" but "a man who has been given a task by a ghost".'[1] As I have suggested, if one amends that to 'a man who has been given a task by his father's ghost', one comes probably as close as one can get, I think, to an adequate formula for the play. On a man profoundly world-weary and melancholy at the death of his father, and even more at the hasty remarriage of his mother, there impinges a revelation and commandment from another world. What, to put it another way, is the 'given' of *Hamlet*? It must surely lie in the combination of the appearance of the Ghost in the first act with what we see of Hamlet in his first scene, the combination of a mysterious and morally indeterminate apparition with a protagonist whose view of life has been soured, perhaps beyond the bounds of reasons, by his mother's frailty. The whole tension of the opening scenes ensures that the Ghost looms before us with extraordinary dramatic force. No other first scene in Shakespeare so excites our attention, with the very feeling of the dark, cold battlements, the stillness of the night, the heart-sickness of the guard. Similarly, in the second scene, Hamlet's first soliloquy is preceded by an extraordinary air of anticipation. Hamlet enters behind the rest of the court (in the Second Quarto stage-direction), dressed in black. His first speeches, cryptic, bitter and satirical, reveal that 'there's something in his soul / O'er which his melancholy sits on brood'. We wait for more to be revealed, and it comes in the first soliloquy.

> That it should come to this:
> But two months dead, nay not so much, not two.
> ...
>
> ...frailty, thy name is woman.
> ...
>
> O, most wicked speed, to post
> With such dexterity to incestuous sheets!
>
> (I.ii. 137–8, 146, 156–7)[2]

These two elements – the Ghost, and Hamlet's disgust – are the elements from which the play takes its beginning. Both are touched with ambiguity: the Ghost is morally ambiguous, and Hamlet's disgust is equally difficult to judge: is it adequately accounted for by the facts, or does it spring from some flaw in the condition of Hamlet's sensibility?

But perhaps the first thing to examine, since it impinges upon us first, is the nature of the Ghost. The idea of the Ghost's moral ambiguity has perhaps already gained some currency, but it may be briefly sketched once again, with some expansion on points which have not received so much attention. Historical critics (E. E. Stoll, J. Dover Wilson, and particularly Eleanor Prosser)[3] have shown that Elizabethan audiences would have responded to the Ghost in a generally suspicious way. But for the reader or spectator of *Hamlet* such external evidence will be important primarily because it reinforces the sense of doubt which already exists in the play itself.

139

Santayana has a suggestive essay on the Ghost and the way in which it serves as a '"point d'appui" for the hero's morbid impulses'.[4] H. A. Mason has written on the suspicious and contradictory presentation of the Ghost in the first act: for him there's no doubt it is something fishy.[5] The words used to describe the Ghost – 'thing', 'dreaded sight', 'apparition', 'illusion', 'like the king' and 'in the same figure like the king that's dead' – all suggest doubt about what the Ghost actually is.

Without spending too much time recapitulating the evidence (that the Ghost 'stalks away' when charged 'by heaven' to speak; that Marcellus says that when the cock crew 'it started like a guilty thing / Upon a fearful summons'), it can simply be recalled that Eleanor Prosser, in her detailed study *Hamlet and Revenge*, has concluded that the Ghost is being presented as something evil. But I would suggest that the evidence is not so conclusive. When the Ghost stalks away it may simply be 'offended' by Horatio's suspicious questions and peremptory demand, rather than being 'chased by the invocation of God'. It appears, at least, in a '*fair* and warlike form'. And one is also impressed by Marcellus's solemn and moving sense of awe at its dignity and ethereality:

> We do it wrong, being so majestical,
> To offer it the show of violence,
> For it is as the air, invulnerable,
> And our vain blows malicious mockery. (I.i. 143–6)

Hamlet's reaction to Horatio's and the soldiers' story at the end of I.ii shows an intense interest, as if it fits in with what he has already been thinking – a second intimation of his 'prophetic soul'. He shares Horatio's suspicions of the Ghost's goodness but is also compelled to seek it out. His first confrontation with it is passionate with doubt and compulsion, but the doubt is evenly balanced between intimations of good and evil ('Be thou a spirit of health or goblin damn'd'). But it is above all the force of Hamlet's reaction that we feel at this point. It is not merely filial duty: his fate cries out. No feeling of his is as indisputable as his passion to question the Ghost. He is at his most courageous, decided, and decisively witty at this moment.

So far then we have responded to the Ghost with a mixture of

140

awe, fear and suspicion, but with riveted attention; above all with a sense of both of its portentousness and its indeterminate nature. The Ghost is a problem both for our perception and for that of the characters.

The moment of Hamlet's confrontation is overwhelming in its drama, and carries the reader or spectator breathlessly to the next scene, so that the Ghost's message falls on Hamlet and us with the force of a revelation. All the more disturbing then is the feeling that the Ghost is not simply a majestic and authoritative figure from another world, and this scene alone should trouble those critics who want to see the Ghost's 'commandment' as conferring an unequivocal duty. Whether or not we feel that the Ghost's account of his torments slips into a grotesque fustian, it is surely indisputable that he is a figure consumed by torments of hatred: he himself says he is condemned to 'fast in fires' until his sins are burned away. He is in a kind of purgatory, and must be seen to be a divided figure. He is divided between a desire for justice and the old taint of hatred and vengeful jealousy, also between his role as an impersonal agent of justice and his feelings of self pity, his desire to exercise a paternal emotional power over his son.

'Pity me not', he says sternly to Hamlet, 'but lend thy serious hearing to what I shall unfold.' He begins then with a tone of calm impersonality and authority. But in his subsequent account of the murder, is he not swayed from this into a violent attack on his wife's sensuality?

> But virtue, as it never will be moved,
> Though lewdness court it in the shape of heaven,
> So lust, though to a radiant angel linked,
> Will sate itself in a celestial bed
> And prey on garbage. (I.v. 53–7)

It is a general pronouncement, but it is difficult not to feel that the Ghost means it to reflect on the particular case; so that 'a radiant angel' becomes touched with elements of self-regard, and Gertrude the personification of lust. And this is not how we see Gertrude in the rest of the play. The Ghost goes on to give an obsessive account of his own poisoning, dwelling almost with fascination on the physical effects of the poisoning and ending in a climax of revulsion.

141

But immediately after this he recovers and speaks in a calmer, more measured and moral tone:

> But howsomever thou pursues this act,
> Taint not thy mind, nor let thy soul contrive
> Against thy mother aught. (ll. 84–6)

It is a wise and, as it turns out, prophetic warning: but has not the Ghost's own narrative up to this point been charged with just those elements which are, if anything is, *likely* to taint Hamlet's mind? Or almost just those elements: one or two other touches ('But soft, methinks I scent the morning air') suggest a freer imagination playing in the interstices of the horror. Is it not possible, then, to see the Ghost as being of a radically divided nature? In which case the 'commandment' enjoined upon Hamlet can also be seen as having a divided nature. On one hand it seems to bear marks of an awesome revelation of truth; on the other it seems to be tainted with corruption.

Hamlet's violent and confused reaction after the Ghost's departing words, his mind reeling from the impact of the relevation, suggests from the first the division in his mind. The Ghost's last words were 'remember me', and it is these words that Hamlet seizes on. But it is worth looking in detail at this speech, in which we see Hamlet's first instinctive reaction to the Ghost's command:

> O all you host of heaven! O earth! What else?
> And shall I couple hell? O fie! Hold, hold, my heart,
> And you, my sinews, grow not instant old,
> But bear me stiffly up. Remember thee?
> Ay, thou poor ghost, whiles memory holds a seat
> In this distracted globe. Remember thee?
> Yea, from the table of my memory
> I'll wipe away all trivial fond records,
> All saws of books, all forms, all pressures past
> That youth and observation copied there,
> And thy commandment all alone shall live
> Within the book and volume of my brain,
> Unmixed with baser matter. Yes, by heaven!
> O most pernicious woman!
> O villain, villain, smiling, damnèd villain!
> My tables – meet it is I set it down
> That one may smile, and smile, and be a villain.

cf. with Richard iii's [?]

At least I am sure it may be so in Denmark.
So, uncle, there you are. Now to my word:
It is 'Adieu, adieu, remember me.'
I have sworn't.   (I.v. 92–112)

The first two lines, with 'heaven' and 'hell', suggest the former doubts in Hamlet's mind – although 'O fie!' could be seen as repudiating the idea that he should 'couple hell'. He feels his physical strength wilt. And then, 'Remember thee?' It is the *remembering* of the Ghost, rather than the command to revenge, that is driven home in this speech: it is this which seems to be the 'commandment' which is all alone to live in Hamlet's brain. And yet having said 'Remember thee?' and repeated it two lines later, Hamlet is immediately seen thinking about something else, firstly Gertrude and then Claudius. No sooner has Hamlet resolved to wipe out of his mind 'all saws of books' than he is noting down on his tablets just one such 'saw' or commonplace observation. What is the significance of this striking contradiction?

It is possible, I think, to explain it as follows. Immediately after his resolve to think of nothing else but 'Remember me', Hamlet is struck by the sudden realization of his mother's guilt, first of all, and then that of Claudius. He is deflected from the Ghost's memory by the sudden sense of the evil with which he is confronted. And then, characteristically, he turns it into a generalization, 'That one may smile...' The generalizing is characteristic (as Coleridge notes several times) but so is the tendency to be deflected from his resolve by his absorption in the evil (as he sees it) with which he is confronted, and particularly, primarily, his mother's guilt. This I think is the main and most obvious sense of the passage. But there is another explanation of his swerving away from the Ghost's 'commandment': that he is unconsciously trying to avoid it, or at least to put it to one side until he has fully taken in the fact of his mother's and uncle's guilt, to fix it in his mind as a fact. The generalization is a part of this effort. But there is something especially characteristic of Hamlet in the flippant qualification, 'At least I am sure it may be so in Denmark.' Hamlet has a sceptical sense of the relativity of human judgement, which runs through the play. When to his 'Denmark's a prison' Rosencrantz replies, 'We think not so my lord', Hamlet retorts, 'Why then 'tis none to you, for there is nothing either good or bad but thinking makes it so.' He is sharply conscious of the fact that our sense of reality depends on our perception. He is ironically saying (of the commonplace 'That one may smile . . . ' etc.), 'At least I'm sure it's true here, in this case', as if to reassure himself. It is as if he stops and focuses on his uncle to get him clearly in view: 'So, uncle, there you are'; and only then can he return to the Ghost's command.

We have here in essence the reaction of Hamlet to the Ghost's command throughout the play: before he can turn to it he has to get Gertrude and Claudius clearly into focus. He has to assure himself of his own perceptions.

The other curious thing about this speech is the Ghost's command itself, not (like the detective story) 'Hamlet, Revenge!', but simply 'Remember me.' Is the Ghost, one might ask, indeed more anxious to be remembered than to be revenged? 'Pity me not', the Ghost has said. And yet its narrative has been one which was particularly likely to arouse Hamlet's pity, and Hamlet returns to the phrase 'poor ghost'. There is a conflict in the Ghost's command between the purely personal nature of its plea for revenge, and the impersonal claim of justice. In so far as the Ghost simply bequeaths to Hamlet an agonizing sense of the evil done to his father, its influence is destructive. The Ghost's paternal authority, reinforced by its supernatural guise, is marked by an egoism which simply seeks control over the son: but on the other hand it is touched also by a sense of impersonal justice. It is, one might say, an image of the authority of the father in general, that authority which, as for Kafka, is at once absurdly human and fallible and at the same time the closest human approximation to the authority of God.

The rest of this scene, which is taken up with the 'cellarage' episode, merely intensifies this sense of the Ghost. Firstly there is Hamlet's wild, perhaps nearly hysterical, foolery as he greets Horatio and Marcellus; his flippant seeming evasion of their questions; his fierce and witty turning on Horatio's quiet attempt to pacify him; and then his request that they swear silence. At the point at which Hamlet holds out his sword for them to swear on, 'the Ghost cries out under the stage' (the stage-direction is in both the Second Quarto and the First Folio). Dover Wilson and Miss Prosser have both noted contemporary parallels in ghost lore strongly

144

suggesting that a spirit who thus appeared would have been regarded as evil, and that there are similar parallels for the phrases Hamlet uses: 'old mole' and 'pioner' in particular.[6] But Hamlet's flippancy or kind of desperate playfulness are elements which cannot be accounted for simply by external evidence, and they seem to be of the essence of this episode:

Ha, ha, boy, say'st thou so? Art thou there truepenny?
Come on. You hear this fellow in the cellarage.
Consent to swear.
. . .
Hic et ubique? Then we'll shift our ground.
. . .
Well said, old mole! Canst work i' th' earth so fast?
A worthy pioner!   (I.v. 150–2, 156, 162–3)

Hamlet's words, and the almost farcical moving about the stage, create an atmosphere of strange, surrealistic comedy, like the comedy of Kafka's 'The Judgement'. They create the feeling that Hamlet is psychologically fencing with the Ghost, holding its authority at a distance, seeking to evade its domination with his taunts and shifting of ground. 'Boy' is disparaging, a term used for servants, and also of course reverses the father–son relationship. Of '*Hic et ubique*' Eleanor Prosser comments that it 'cannot refer to an "honest ghost", for only God and the devil can be here and everywhere at the same time' (p. 140). But if *both* powers have this attribute Miss Prosser's inference is illogical. The phrase, in its double reference, illustrates in fact the essential ambiguity of the Ghost, the way in which it carries connotations of both heaven and hell. The last remark of Hamlet is almost jocularly patronizing, as if he is tempering the Ghost's authority by metaphorically clapping him on the back.

All this adds up to a strong feeling of irony and moral uncertainty about a Ghost who is also a father's ghost. It is in this episode that Hamlet falls spontaneously into the 'antic disposition' that at the close of the scene he says he is going to put on. One may, therefore, see Hamlet's assumed (or half-assumed) moments of madness as springing directly from this episode. They are the stratagem of a mind at odds with itself and its own perceptions, and radically uncertain about the authority behind the 'duty' imposed upon it.

By means of this stratagem Hamlet will hide himself from the outside world while trying to bring himself and others more clearly into focus.

II

The ambiguities of our perception of the Ghost coincide with those of our perception of Hamlet himself, and for similar reasons. When we first see Hamlet (in I.ii.) he is a melancholy, embittered outsider in a court which is, outwardly at least, harmonious, orderly and presided over by a dignified king. Whether we are immediately to take Hamlet's part does not seem clear: the case has been argued exhaustively on both sides, the romantic view seeing him as a solitary hero in the midst of a corrupt court,[7] and a characteristic modern view perceiving Hamlet as a sick soul in a surrounding atmosphere of light, air, and warm humanity.[8] When we see or read through the play it is probably difficult to commit ourselves to either view exclusively. Hamlet's first remarks must be baffling to us unless we look further ahead to explain them. And his speech about his inner grief could well seem a piece of bragging self-righteousness. 'Why seems it [the knowledge of death] so particular with thee', says the Queen; and Hamlet:

> Seems, madam? Nay, it is. I know not 'seems'.
> 'Tis not alone my inky cloak, good mother,
> Nor customary suits of solemn black,
> Nor windy suspiration of forced breath,
> No, nor the fruitful river in the eye,
> Nor the dejected haviour of the visage,
> Together with all forms, moods, shapes of grief,
> That can denote me truly. These indeed seem,
> For these are actions that a man might play,
> But I have that within which passes show;
> These but the trappings and the suits of woe. (I.ii. 76–86)

Hamlet is very sure that he knows not 'seems', and that he knows what 'is', but the rest of the play does not bear him out. For a long time he does not seem to know what he himself is. Even in the specific matter of grief for his father, the speech itself shows him less sure of reality than he thinks, for the main feeling behind this speech is not so much grief, as *indignation*. The speech itself contradicts what it claims to say: 'I have that within', but it is a

146

very flamboyant and public demonstration of it. 'These are actions that a man might play', but Hamlet himself is being histrionic about his repudiation of them. 'I have that within' is a very sonorous claim, but it risks sounding ridiculous, rather like 'Well, I know what I mean.' Hamlet is claiming an inner reality and identity which (like a sulky child) he is not going to show anyone else. But as a result the audience does not see it either, and it is only a romantic view which simply takes Hamlet at his own valuation.

Like the court, we are wondering what is the matter with Hamlet, and the whole scene is calculated to keep us wondering until the other characters leave the stage and Hamlet is left alone. Then we find out. Hamlet is close to despair because of the speed of his mother's remarriage. We witness a powerful reaction to human fallibility, particularly sexual fallibility. But there is also the sense of a violence of reaction that owes something of its intensity to a particular quality in the speaker himself. 'O, that this too too solid flesh would melt': Hamlet feels that the taint is in his *own* nature (and the Second Quarto reading of 'sallied' or 'sullied' clearly reinforces this if we take that version). We can, I think, agree with L. C. Knights when he says that 'what we have to take note of is not only what he says but a peculiar vibration in the saying'.[9] And the vibration is most marked in Hamlet's emphasis on the sexual motive in his mother's remarriage:

> O, most wicked speed, to post
> With such dexterity to incestuous sheets,   (I.ii. 156–7)

where it seems it is the dexterity that appals Hamlet as much as the incest. One treads here on difficult ground, but those critics seem to me in a general way right who see Hamlet's disgust as springing from something in his own nature as well as from something in the outside world. Like the Ghost, Hamlet is divided between nobility and corruption, and sexual feeling is the focus of this division.

The bitter colloquy with Ophelia in III.i has long provided difficulties of textual and dramatic interpretation, but however we resolve these the scene remains a disturbing one, particularly for those who would emphasize Hamlet's nobility. The same corrosive sense of disillusionment with human relationships breathes through the scene as in the soliloquy just commented on. And one might look

147

back briefly to what seems to me a very significant moment in charting the soul-progress of a man who has just seen a ghost: the relation by Ophelia in II.i of Hamlet's visit to her. The scene follows that in which Hamlet sees the Ghost, the brief preceding matter being the conversation between Polonius and Reynaldo. If we seek out minutely for clues to the time sequence we discover that Hamlet's visit occurred two months after the ghostly meeting; and yet this seems immaterial in the actual experiencing of the play, where Hamlet seems to have gone straight from the battlements to Ophelia's closet, looking 'As if he had been loosed out of hell / To speak of horrors'. The feeling we receive in the theatre or as we read through the play is that the Hamlet described here is still reeling from his encounter with the Ghost. His intense and protracted scrutiny of Ophelia, as if seeking out her very reality, suggests a questioning of her nature directly prompted by the Ghost's emphasis on Gertrude's infidelity and sensuality.[10]

The questioning scrutiny turns to verbal questioning in III.i. But before looking at the episode with Ophelia we must examine the famous soliloquy that precedes it. Indeed the two things are not often put together, whereas in the play the caustic and even savage behaviour to Ophelia follows directly on the inner musing.

> To be, or not to be: that is the question:
> Whether 'tis nobler in the mind to suffer
> The slings and arrows of outrageous fortune,
> Or to take arms against a sea of troubles,
> And by opposing end them. To die, to sleep –
> No more – and by a sleep to say we end
> The heartache and the thousand natural shocks
> That flesh is heir to! 'Tis a consummation
> Devoutly to be wished. To die, to sleep –
> To sleep – perchance to dream: ay, there's the rub,
> For in that sleep of death what dreams may come
> When we have shuffled off this mortal coil,
> Must give us pause. There's the respect
> That makes calamity of so long life:
> For who would bear the whips and scorns of time,
> Th' oppressor's wrong, the proud man's contumely,
> The pangs of despised love, the law's delay,
> The insolence of office, and the spurns
> That patient merit of th'unworthy takes,
> When he himself might his quietus make

148

With a bare bodkin? Who would fardels bear,
To grunt and sweat under a weary life,
But that the dread of something after death,
The undiscovered country from whose bourn
No traveller returns, puzzles the will,
And makes us rather bear those ills we have,
Than fly to others that we know not of?
Thus conscience doth make cowards of us all,
And thus the native hue of resolution
Is sicklied o'er with the pale cast of thought,
And enterprises of great pitch and moment,
With this regard their currents turn awry,
And lose the name of action. – Soft you now,
The fair Ophelia! – Nymph, in thy orisons
Be all my sins remembered.   (III.i. 56–90)

I would suggest that the most striking thing about this soliloquy is
its irrelevance to Hamlet's predicament: not only in the pains of life
Hamlet describes which have nothing to do with his own – the
pangs of despised love, the law's delay etc. – and in the total
forgetfulness that he has met a traveller from the undiscovered
country, but also in the whole musing on death. It is firstly difficult
enough to say what the speech actually means. Is Hamlet mainly
wondering 'Whether 'tis nobler...'; is it *nobility* of action or
suffering he is concerned with? Or is he preoccupied mainly with
a fear of what comes after death? (Middleton Murry asks this
question.)[11] Does the 'being' of the first line refer to whether or not
we will 'be' after death, or to some existential kind of 'being' which
may be achieved either by action or suffering? Is there any
parallelism, as there would seem to be from the rhythm and syntax,
between 'To be...' and 'Whether 'tis nobler in the mind...', and
'or not to be' and 'Or to take arms...'? 'To be' would then be 'to
suffer', and 'not to be' would be to act and die. And yet in D. H.
Lawrence's suggestive reading of the phrase the correlation is
between 'to be' and 'to take arms' – to be the king, in the life of
the body – and between 'not to be' and 'to suffer...', which is the
way of Christian negation (see above, pp. 81–3). The gnomic
quality of the line and what follows has a kind of ambiguity which
blurs the sense rather than adding a richness of multiple meanings.
And yet the fame of the passage must have something to do with
the fact that one can find all these meanings there, and which one

149

one finds depends on one's point of view, one's reading of the play as a whole. But viewed dispassionately, the speech, like the play, is a puzzle. Nor can it tell us anything decisive about Hamlet's 'character' or even his ideas at this point in the play. All it tells us is that his mind is wandering, though wandering over some interesting country. Dr Johnson was right to say that the continuity of the speech is not in the speaker's words; but his assumption that it was behind the words in some way, and in Hamlet's thought, is questionable.[12] His paraphrase in his Notes on the play makes the speech intelligible, but it is not what Hamlet says, and other paraphrases are equally defensible or indefensible. In the end they are indefensible because they rewrite the speech. Hamlet's preoccupations stay in our minds, but not the connection between them. 'To be or not to be' – it is the phrase which stays in the mind. Hamlet is preoccupied with *being*, with how to be, how to act so as to 'become himself'. As in Kafka's aphorism (see above, p. 121), to act may be to destroy himself, which leads him to thoughts of death. But he can connect nothing with nothing. His speech drifts away from the debate between being and not being, between action and suffering, into scruples about death, which have nothing to do with nobility. The speech enacts Hamlet's 'pale cast of thought' in the way it loses the emphatic quality of its opening. 'To be or not to be' feels like the prelude to a resolution, but the resolve never comes. It begins by taking on the problem of being, of acting or suffering, of achieving an identity; but drifts off into the speculation of an uncertain perception. It pulls the wool over Hamlet's own eyes because it seems to follow logically from the opening 'question', but does not do so.

The speech begins as if with the prelude to a resolution; it ends with the fear of death, and with Hamlet's 'sins'. There is a connection here: it can only be guilt which makes Hamlet fear death and 'what dreams may come', and so he closes with his quiet wish for Ophelia's prayers. Hamlet's dread of death is a dread of what he *is* (which would determine 'what dreams may come'). As in Kierkegaard, his dread of death is the dread of the possibility of guilt (see above, p. 93). This sense of guilt is one of the dominant things in Hamlet's mind in the subsequent dialogue with Ophelia, and is

150

the quality which connects the conversation with the soliloquy. For as well as attacking Ophelia in this scene Hamlet attacks himself.

> Get thee to a nunnery. Why wouldst thou be a breeder of sinners? I am myself indifferent honest, but yet I could accuse me of such things it were better my mother had not borne me: I am very proud, revengeful, ambitious, with more offences at my beck than I have thoughts to put them in, imagination to give them shape, or time to act them in. What should such fellows as I do, crawling between earth and heaven? We are arrant knaves all; believe none of us. Go thy ways to a nunnery. Where's your father?
>
> (III.i. 121–31)

The self-criticisms are vehement, but the specific faults – 'proud, revengeful, ambitious' – do not seem particularly apt. (Elsewhere Hamlet is criticizing himself for not being revengeful enough.) Yet one feels that Hamlet sees them as potentially there. Like Stephen Dedalus at one point in *A Portrait of the Artist* he feels that he is guilty of *all* kinds of sin.[13] This is one of the aspects of what Kierkegaard calls 'dread', a fear of what the self may become, and therefore what it potentially already is. Dread could be described as a fear of 'identity'. Hamlet does not know who or what he is, and nor can we understand his 'character'. Whether Hamlet is the 'sweet prince' or 'arrant knave' is never resolved by the play – unless we can sense, like Mallarmé, that Hamlet's nobility is 'le joyau intacte sous le désastre' (see above, p. 25). At the end of this scene there is Ophelia's soliloquy, 'O what a noble mind is here o'erthrown.' It is a curiously stilted speech (as someone has said, like a *Times* obituary), so that perhaps it does not carry very much weight in our total impression of Hamlet. It refers (like Bradley and other critics who make so much of what Hamlet was like before the play begins) to things which we do not see, or only fleetingly, in the play. But we see something of them: the courtier's ease and *sprezzatura* of Hamlet with the Players, the scholar's reading and pondering, the soldier's 'continual practice' at swordsmanship; not to mention Hamlet's genuine love of Horatio, his openness and generosity. Are these perhaps enough to lodge with us a sense of Mallarmé's 'joyau'?

There is also the element in this scene of Hamlet's trying to act as a kind of moral authority. What he thinks he can teach Ophelia is obscure, and one might think he is just talking to himself. But he seems to be also trying to warn Ophelia of certain realities of which she is unaware. He may of course also be half-aware of her possible duplicity. 'Get thee to a nunnery' is a kind of bitter warning as well as a misplaced criticism of Ophelia. He identifies her with his idea of 'woman' in general and irrationally says things to her which spring clearly from thoughts prompted by what the Ghost has said about Gertrude. But he is also trying to tell her what he thinks about himself. There is a kind of desperate naïvety about this, and self-pity. 'We are arrant knaves all; believe none of us.' Hamlet is close here to the complaining, fretful anti-hero of Laforgue's poems. But there is no doubt that both of them feel they have something to say about life and experience.

There are other places where Hamlet sets about educating people. One is the scene with Rosencrantz and Guildenstern (ii.ii). The other is iii.iv, the scene with Gertrude. Since the latter is rather like the scene with Ophelia, in that it is full of Hamlet's self-righteous moral criticism, it had best be considered here. As in the earlier scene, Hamlet seems torn between his own obsessions and his desire to warn and teach. He begins his upbraiding passionately, but with control, though somewhat pompously ('Such an act / That blurs the grace and blush of modesty'). But in the next speech, which comes notably when he is comparing the *pictures* of his father and uncle, he moves towards a criticism which concentrates exclusively on her sensuality, rather than her breaking of faith with old Hamlet. His language becomes very fustian and overblown ('Rebellious hell / If thou canst mutine in a matron's bones / To flaming youth let virtue be as wax' etc.) and ends by breaking out in an obsessive and tainted language:

> Nay, but to live
> In the rank sweat of an enseamèd bed,
> Stewed in corruption, honeying and making love
> Over the nasty sty...   (iii.iv. 92–5)

The reappearance of the Ghost at the end of this speech must be considered later. But for the moment it is the division in Hamlet between obsessive disgust and moral lucidity that must be mainly

152

noted. Bradley seems to be finely perceptive when he notes how, after the disappearance of the Ghost and after Gertrude's 'O Hamlet, thou hast cleft my heart in twain', Hamlet breaks out with

> O, throw away the worser part of it,
> And live the purer with the other half.   (ll. 158–9)

Hamlet does not lose his moral sense in the scene, despite the prevalence of his obsessive sexual disgust and a kind of desire for verbal revenge. He seems to be trying to separate the two and achieve a kind of moral authority.

III

Questions of perception, authority and identity are not in the end separable in the experience of the play. How Hamlet sees the Ghost is connected with how he sees himself, and both in turn contribute to his sense of his own identity and ultimately to our sense of it. His own attempts to speak as a kind of authority to Ophelia and Gertrude are also a part of his attempt to see, and to understand himself.

But as important as this question of seeing and understanding is the question of feeling. This I think accounts for much of the significance of Hamlet's relationship with the Players; and it is that part of the play, together with the ensuing Play-scene, that I propose to examine next. Polonius says that there was 'a kind of joy' in Hamlet to hear of the arrival of the Players, and we indeed see this 'joy' in his free and open behaviour with them. 'Joy' is a striking quality to attribute to Hamlet, but perhaps it is warranted. In the Players, whom Hamlet treats very much as old friends, we see men whose profession it is to assume identities. That ability which Hamlet finds so difficult in his own life, the Players achieve in the special conditions of their art. Hamlet says that one can see in them 'the very age and body of the time his form and pressure', as even more than in the words of the dramatist we *see* reality embodied in the actor of the drama. This confers a particular dignity on the art of acting. Hamlet's enthusiasm in giving advice to the actors is an enthusiasm for an art which is in a special sense an art of 'being'.

Perception, authority, and identity: a reading

The strong impression made on him by the First Player's speech is the impression made by someone who can feel, and 'be' someone else through the means of art.

What Hamlet dislikes more than anything is overacting.

Be not too tame neither, but let your own discretion be your tutor. Suit the action to the word, the word to the action, with this special observance, that you o'erstep not the modesty of nature. For anything so o'erdone is from the very purpose of playing, whose end, both at the first and now, was and is, to hold, as 'twere, the mirror up to nature; to show virtue her own feature, scorn her own image, and the very age and body of the time his form and pressure. (III.ii. 17–25)

The integrity of action and word, word and action, has a special appeal to Hamlet, and obviously relates to his sense of his own incapacities, not only with regard to his task, but also to his general behaviour. For he is of course particularly prone to overacting: the scene at Ophelia's burial springs most readily to mind, but one can take an example closer to this part of the play, his soliloquy after his first meeting with the Players and his listening to the First Player's Priam speech.

The Player's speech has obvious bearing on Hamlet's predicament. It is about the death of Priam beneath the revenging sword of Pyrrhus and about Hecuba's grief for Priam: about revenge, and the grief of a wife for the death of her husband. But it is not so much that aspect which Hamlet concentrates on as the fact of the Player's emotional response to what he is reciting.

> O, what a rogue and peasant slave am I!
> Is it not monstrous that this player here,
> But in a fiction, in a dream of passion,
> Could force his soul so to his own conceit
> That from her working all his visage wanned,
> Tears in his eyes, distraction in his aspect,
> A broken voice, and his whole function suiting
> With forms to his conceit? And all for nothing!
> For Hecuba!
> What's Hecuba to him, or he to Hecuba,
> That he should weep for her? What would he do
> Had he the motive and the cue for passion
> That I have? He would drown the stage with tears
> And cleave the general ear with horrid speech,
> Make mad the guilty and appal the free,

154

Perception, authority, and identity: a reading

Confound the ignorant, and amaze indeed
The very faculties of eyes and ears.
Yet I,
A dull and muddy mettled rascal, peak
Like John a'dreams, unpregnant of my cause,
And can say nothing. No, not for a king,
Upon whose property and most dear life
A damned defeat was made. Am I a coward?
Who calls me villain? Breaks my pate across?
Plucks off my beard and blows it in my face?
Tweaks me by the nose? Gives me the lie i' the throat
As deep as to the lungs? Who does me this?
Ha, 'swounds, I should take it, for it cannot be
But I am pigeon-livered and lack gall
To make oppression bitter, or ere this
I should have fatted all the region kites
With this slave's offal. Bloody, bawdy villain,
Remorseless, treacherous, lecherous, kindless villain!
O, vengeance!   (ii.ii. 560–93)

There is perhaps a question whether Hamlet wholly admires the Player's performance, since he calls it 'monstrous' that he can work up such passion. Yet at the end of the speech he has said ''Tis well', and the main impression here is that Hamlet sees real feeling in the Player, which contrasts with his own lack of feeling. He raises the possibility that it may be accounted for in almost physical terms, that he lacks 'gall'. It is a lack of some kind of essential being. Yet it is odd that he should say that he can 'say nothing' since he is saying such a lot, and since indeed he goes on to see this as part of the problem, that he

> Must, like a whore, unpack my heard with words
> And fall a-cursing like a very drab,
> A stallion!   (ll. 597–9)

The point is, presumably, that speech and the expression of passion can be the enemies of action as well as its concomitants. Only when speech comes out of some essential integrity of being, and is itself a kind of action, is it creative (as the words of love are creative as opposed to the words of the 'drab'). The soliloquy as a whole enacts as well as describes Hamlet's predicament; it is itself a symptom of his condition. The language of

155

> drown the stage with tears
> And cleave the general ear with horrid speech (ll. 572–3)

is already inflated currency. And in

> Plucks off my beard and blows it in my face?
> Tweaks me by the nose? (ll. 584–5)

there is almost a lapse into hysterical flippancy since hyperbole can go no further. The style itself is a symptom of Hamlet's inability to 'be'. One can admit a slightly different interpretation of the tone, which is perhaps more attractive since it preserves Hamlet's awareness of the situation, by invoking irony: 'drown the stage with tears' would then have overtones of criticism of the already overstated nature of the Player's performance; and 'Tweaks me by the nose' would have a conscious wittiness about it. But the idea of Hamlet's enactment of his own inadequacy would remain the same: it would simply be that Hamlet was ironically guying his own tendency to exaggerate, would in a sense be underplaying his feelings by means of irony, rather than overplaying them.

But the underlying idea is that the Player can 'suit the action to the word, the word to the action', and Hamlet cannot. The Players delight him as artists of the 'being' which he himself cannot attain. Even in this speech Hamlet is merely 'observing himself' in Kafka's phrase, rather than exercising that active self-knowledge which would lead to self-judgement and 'making of himself what he is' (see above, p. 121).

In his advice to the Players Hamlet says it offends him to the soul to hear a fellow 'tear a passion to tatters', but he does it himself in the climax to this speech. He also says 'Let those that play your clowns speak no more than is set down for them.' Could one perhaps relate this, too, to Hamlet himself? His tendency to repeat words was noted as particularly characteristic by Bradley. But the examples come only in the Folio text and not in the Second Quarto. This suggests at least the possibility that it was the actor who performed Hamlet who added the repetitions, and that these were incorporated in the Folio version which for many reasons is often regarded as representing a text taken from performance. The repetitions might be the actor's intensification of a tendency in Hamlet's character to inflate the currency of words, or conversely to gain intensity by

156

repetition. One can imagine Hamlet as being aware of this tendency in himself and this being related to his concern with speaking to the text (or to the matter) in his advice to the clowns. Hamlet often speaks 'more than is set down for him', in a metaphorical sense; and perhaps the actor did this literally with the text, either in the heat of the moment or by design. The point is also one more illustration of Hamlet as clown: the Hamlet close to Laforgue or Prufrock.

IV

After the part of the soliloquy which has just been examined, Hamlet goes on to set his brains to work and comes up with the idea of the Mousetrap. The idea of the play grows directly out of his preoccupation with the Player's emotion and his own lack of 'gall'. He voices another doubt about the Ghost ('The spirit I have seen may be the devil'), but concludes that the play will decide the matter. It is a device of the plot, but it also has other kinds of significance. First of all it is surely significant that Hamlet chooses to test the word of the Ghost by becoming an *author*. The use of the Mousetrap could be seen as an image of the function of art in general: by its means men can test the reality of their imaginings and distinguish between illusion and reality. 'The poet and the dreamer are distinct', wrote Keats, 'Diverse, sheer opposite, antipodes'. Hamlet has had 'bad dreams'. To test (perhaps) their correspondence to reality, Hamlet puts on a play. He has said that the purpose of playing is 'to hold a mirror up to nature', which can mean both to reflect Nature merely, and also to allow it to see itself. From the play of the four Worthies in *Love's Labour's Lost* to the masques of *The Tempest* Shakespeare is frequently preoccupied with the power of drama, and in his later years particularly its power to influence men's behaviour. Hamlet has a strong and unusual belief in its efficacy.

> I have heard that guilty creatures sitting at a play
> Have by the very cunning of the scene
> Been struck so to the soul that presently
> They have proclaimed their malefactions.   (II.ii. 601–4)

Taken literally this is perhaps a primitive idea and posits a primitive audience. But the idea that drama might have the power to make vice more conscious of itself, and hence more likely to reform, or

157

expose itself as guilt, is not so primitive. Hamlet is planning to hold the mirror up to the King and to see if he sees himself. He is also holding a mirror up to himself (which may be one of the reasons he makes the murderer Lucianus 'nephew to the King'). Hamlet will also test himself by looking in the mirror. Like Mallarmé's Igitur he will see his own 'character' (*personnage*) in the mirror, with its destructive egoism, its evil (personified in Lucianus); and will see it disappear as, with the King's revelation of his own guilt, Lucianus becomes not the reflection of Hamlet, the potential murderer of a king, but Claudius, the man who has already murdered a king. Lucianus is potentially a mirror image of either Claudius or Hamlet; if the King reveals his guilt the reflection of Hamlet will disappear.

The play then will be a means of establishing the identity of Hamlet and Claudius: a tool of perception.

What the Mousetrap proves, if anything, is therefore crucial to our sense of Hamlet, Claudius and the Ghost. And here I would like to try and draw on a recent study of the Play-scene. In his essay, 'Did the King See the Dumb Show?', W. W. Robson has argued for 'a *quiet* treatment' of the scene.[14] The main problem of the scene for the spectator is to decide how decisively the King reveals his guilt. Professor Robson suggests that the evidence is not conclusive. The King's behaviour resolves Hamlet's doubt on this point 'without resolving the doubt of the thoughtful spectator'. The evidence put forward for this interpretation is firstly the fact that the King does not react to the Dumb Show. There have been many previous attempts to get round this problem (like Dover Wilson's stratagem of having the King not see the Dumb Show) but it is true that none of them seems entirely satisfactory. We know of course (if we ever doubted) that the King has committed murder, because of his guilty aside in a previous scene; and if any doubt lingers in our minds it is dispelled in the prayer scene. The question is, I take it, does the King react to the specific details of the crime depicted in the Mousetrap? The most common view is that while the king realizes that Hamlet knows his secret and the details of the murder, he manages to steel himself to sit through the Dumb Show, but can hold out no longer when the play itself presents the same incidents again, and these are intensified by Hamlet's comments. Professor Robson's view on the other hand amounts to suggesting that the

King does not fully recognize his crime in the details of the Dumb Show, and leaves, sternly but by no means in a panic, only when Hamlet's remarks appear pointedly aimed at himself and the Queen.

The implications of this are large. If the King sees the Dumb Show but does not recognize his crime, doubt is immediately thrown on the Ghost's narration. Apart from the present context, the poisoning in the ear strikes Professor Robson as distinctly odd, even though it was an 'Italianate' crime of a kind recorded in contemporary stories. It is particularly lurid, perhaps physically implausible, and it has an undeniable sexual symbolism. Robson mentions a drawing by Fuseli. One might also recall at this point D. H. Lawrence's idea of the puritan 'recoil' from sexuality brought on by the introduction of syphilis into England in the sixteenth century. The poisoning in the ear and the Ghost's account of the physical effects of the poison might easily suggest venereal disease (see above, p. 85). The implication is, I think, that the Ghost's account of its death is distorted by its sexual jealousy. One might add to this the idea that the Ghost is conceivably, in part, Hamlet's own creation. Horatio and the soldiers also see the Ghost, but only Hamlet hears it speak, and in order to get it to speak he partly confers on it an identity.

> I'll call thee Hamlet,
> King, father, royal Dane. O, answer me!   (I.iv. 44–5)

The fact that the Ghost and Hamlet share a similar kind of language and similar kinds of obsession suggests too, though faintly, that what the Ghost *says* may in part be a creation of Hamlet's mind, and that the details of the murder and the poisoning are as well.

But this last point may be overstating the case, or digging right through the bottom of the play, and readers who find it wildly speculative and unfounded can abandon it at once if they wish, and if thereby they retain the patience to follow what I think is the main argument. This is that the king's behaviour does not *prove* that he is reacting to the detailed presentation of his own crime and to Hamlet's evident knowledge of those details. Let us look at the moment when he rises and leaves the play. (I am still broadly following Professor Robson's account as I understand it, with one or two added suggestions which I shall indicate.) The moment occurs

159

like this. As, on the court stage, Lucianus pours the poison into the ear of the Player King, Hamlet says

> 'A poisons him i' th' garden for his estate. His name's Gonzago.
> The story is extant, and written in very choice Italian. You shall
> see anon how the murderer gets the love of Gonzago's wife.
>
> *Ophelia.* The King rises.
> *Hamlet.* What, frighted with false fire?
> *Queen.* How fares my lord?
> *Polonius.* Give o'er the play.
> *King.* Give me some light. Away!
> *Polonius.* Lights, lights, lights!
> [*Exeunt all but* Hamlet *and* Horatio.]
>
> (III.ii. 267–76)

It is clear that the King rises not 'on the talk of the poisoning' but at the moment of the insult to the Queen. The King cannot fail to feel the weight of Hamlet's innuendoes, but what does he *reveal*? To the court his departure would simply reveal his displeasure at the tastelessness of the play and the rudeness of Hamlet's innuendoes, particularly to the Queen. I would add to Robson's account here the following point: The court (who were all there in I.ii) know Hamlet's antipathy to the King and to the remarriage. It is this that they would primarily see behind Hamlet's enigmatic remarks. But do we the audience see him any differently? We virtually know he is a murderer, but that is different from saying that he reveals it at this point. He seems to leave calmly, while Polonius fusses.

It is also striking, as Professor Robson points out, that, in his soliloquy during the prayer-scene, Claudius makes no reference to the fact that Hamlet has discovered his crime. This surely would have astounded him, had he been struck by it and surprised into a flustered retreat, so that he would almost have been bound to mention it. It is only negative evidence, but it might suggest again that the King does not think 'Hamlet has learned about my crime' because he has not seen the details of it in the Mousetrap. He might simply suspect that Hamlet had either got wind of the murder in a general way or was simply throwing out uncannily accurate guesses at what happened.

I am aware here that I am drawing out conclusions in a speculative form in a way that Professor Robson to a great extent avoids. I am also aware that I am steering close to what Waldock

160

called 'the documentary fallacy', the critical procedure which treats the play as if it were a piece of history with motives to be investigated and other 'facts' to be discovered. But it seems to me that some such imaginative latitude must be allowed the reader or audience if they are to make sense of a play at all. We must often infer what has happened in the plot of a play from what is implied but not stated. To take one example from a different play: when Lady Macbeth says to Macbeth in I.vii, 'What beast was't, then, / That made you break this enterprise to me?', we have to infer either that she is lying or deceiving herself by saying that it was Macbeth who first broached the idea of the murder of Duncan; or that somewhere in the time after I.v, when Macbeth and his wife were to 'speak further' of the witches' prophecy, Macbeth spoke to his wife of the 'thought' whose 'murder yet [was] but fantastical' in I.iv. It is a significant matter about which there is no unequivocal evidence. Perhaps Shakespeare was content for us to make the latter inference, which is the more obvious. Or perhaps he deliberately left this crucial incident to happen off stage, so that the impression we get is of evil's having grown mysteriously from the 'imaginings' of both protagonists. In either case the unstated implication is important in our response to the play. *Hamlet*, more perhaps than any other of Shakespeare's plays, puts us in situations where we have to draw conclusions which are not stated in the play's text. Waldock was right to draw attention to this and to the fact that critics have drifted away from large areas of what is given in the play and filled up gaps with their own inventions. But the play itself almost invites us to do this: it is a kind of puzzle designed to exercise our perception. A successful criticism of the play would have to keep a constant tension between the speeches and actions that are there before us, and the dimensions behind themselves they must inevitably suggest.

There is enough in this scene to suggest that Professor Robson is right to find the King's departure less than a revelation of his guilt. Hamlet, on the other hand, seems, on the face of it, convinced.

Hamlet. O good Horatio, I'll take the ghost's word for a thousand pound. Didst perceive?
Horatio. Very well, my lord.
Hamlet. Upon the talk of the poisoning?
Horatio. I did very well note him.　　　　　　　　(III.ii. 292–6)

But it was not, as I have suggested, on the talk of the poisoning that the King *rose*, whatever expression his face may have shown. Horatio obviously noted something, but is tantalizingly unforthcoming about *what* he noted and even more so about what conclusions he draws from what he saw. And Hamlet's reaction is curiously flippant (as Robson notes in passing). His first reaction, indeed, was his elated little rhyme and his joke about becoming a playwright (or perhaps actor) – one of the clues for Laforgue's version of the character in his *Moralité* (see above, p. 37). There is a suspicion here that he is not sobered and resolved by the confirmation of the Ghost's word, but headily elated, and still playing a kind of role. In the terms in which I am considering the play, if his perception had become finally clarified by the King's behaviour his sense of himself would have immediately become clarified too, whereas perhaps there is a little more than simple fooling in his 'Would not this, sir...get me a fellowship in a cry of players?' There is a kind of irony in it which harks back to his involvement with the Players and his half-grudging admiration of the reality in the First Player's Priam speech, a kind of ironic sense that he is still 'acting' here.

One can, I think, therefore conclude that the Mousetrap has not proved anything, but left matters deliberately undecided. What I take to be Professor Robson's fundamental idea that our perspective on the Play-scene need not be the same as Hamlet's seems to me highly suggestive. It suggests that the Ghost must remain morally ambiguous, and that Hamlet has not gained grounds for new certainty. The mirror which Hamlet holds up to the King, and up to himself, remains blurred, and Lucianus the murderer has as much the lineaments of the nephew Hamlet as of the brother Claudius. Hamlet is no closer to a correct perception of the Ghost's authority or of his own identity, and we the audience are no closer either. But at the same time our perception is different from Hamlet's because unlike him we are aware of another way of seeing Claudius's behaviour, and are aware of a lack of substance in Hamlet's immediate response to the events.

V

What do subsequent events add to our sense of the Ghost and of Hamlet's perception of it? There is the Ghost's third appearance on stage, in the scene of Hamlet's interview with his mother, but apart from his response to it there, Hamlet does not mention the Ghost again, even in soliloquy. On the other hand, what changes do we see taking place in Hamlet himself? Do we see him gaining in any kind of moral certainty or behaving with less randomness and strangeness than we did before? It is these questions, taking the play from the Play-scene to the end of IV.v (the last time we see Hamlet until after his voyage and return), that must be considered next.

At the end of III.ii. Hamlet has a soliloquy which is at least curious coming from one who has supposedly just proved the honesty of the Ghost and might now be expected to achieve a calmer resolve.

> 'Tis now the very witching time of night,
> When churchyards yawn, and hell itself breathes out
> Contagion to this world. Now could I drink hot blood
> And do such bitter business as the day
> Would quake to look on.   (ll. 396–400)

It is strange that Hamlet should still be thinking of yawning churchyards and of hell – unless we entertain the idea that his taking the Ghost's word was not a very deep resolve, and that his imagination still couples revenants from the dead with evil. (H. A. Mason notes in another connection that in I.iv Hamlet refers to the Ghost as if it were a *corpse* which the grave has cast up again.) 'Now could I drink hot blood' is, moreover, pure revenge melodrama. The soliloquy goes on to speak of Gertrude: immediately after the Play-scene, then, Hamlet is absorbed again with the question of his mother; admittedly she sends for him, but he is clearly ready to let himself be deflected from his 'course' ('If he but blench I know my course').

On his way to the Queen he comes upon the King praying.

> Now might I do it pat, now 'a is a-praying
> And now I'll do it.   (III.iii. 73–4)

163

But he does not, and the reason, whatever it is, must be crucial for our interpretation of the play. Coleridge and Bradley both explained the speech as a kind of excuse or rationalization of (respectively) his 'pale cast of thought' and his melancholy. This does seem to take the technique of looking for a character's meaning behind his words, rather than in them, considerably too far. Dr Johnson was surely right when he said that Hamlet is saying just what he means, and that the speech is horrifying. It cannot but turn Hamlet into an evil avenger, at least at this moment. But certain details of the speech suggest more than this, and indicate by what psychological process Hamlet comes to this state of mind.

> 'A took my father grossly, full of bread,
> With all his crimes broad blown, as flush as May;
> And how his audit stands, who knows save heaven?
> But in our circumstance and course of thought,
> 'Tis heavy with him. (ll. 80–4)

At the moment when he might have killed the King, Hamlet is restrained by the memory of the Ghost's account of its suffering. 'With all his crimes broad blown, as flush as May': it is a very different picture from Hamlet's customary idealization of his father, and can only come from the Ghost's account of its death and purgatorial suffering. And indeed Hamlet's words recall the precise image used by the Ghost to describe its state of soul at death,

> Cut off even in the blossoms of my sin,
> Unhouseled, disappointed, unaneled,
> No reck'ning made, but sent to my account
> With all my imperfections on my head. (i.v. 76–9)

Would it not be true to say that Hamlet's mind has been tainted with its horrifying vindictiveness precisely because of the Ghost's description of its own suffering? The moment here at which Hamlet might have said to the King, 'Face your death. I come to execute you for the murder of my father', he is betrayed into this state of vindictiveness by the memory of the Ghost. The Ghost's memory, which should be a spur to justice, is also a snare. The authority of the Ghost, even after Hamlet is convinced he has proved its honesty, is unavoidably compromised by its human frailty. Hamlet's perception of it can never separate the two elements.

In a similar way, in the scene with Gertrude, Hamlet's language is full of those metaphors of disease for which we can find an origin in the Ghost's original account of its poisoning. H. D. F. Kitto sees the evil in the play spreading from Claudius's original crime until it taints even Hamlet.[15] But Claudius's crime is not the opening of the play. And the continuity of the language of Hamlet's speech above and in III.iv with the language of the Ghost suggests another source of the evil.

But why, in this scene, does the Ghost appear again? He gives us a reason,

> Do not forget. This visitation
> Is but to whet thy almost blunted purpose, (ll. 111–12)

but why does he appear precisely at this moment? If the Ghost had encountered Hamlet immediately after the prayer-scene it would have been more appropriate for this message. Clearly his return must also have something to do with the presence of Gertrude and Hamlet's berating of her. Hamlet has just been building up to a climax of hatred against Claudius:

> Hamlet.　　　A murderer and a villain,
> A slave that is not twentieth part the tithe
> Of your precedent lord, a vice of kings,
> A cutpurse of the empire and the rule,
> That from a shelf the precious diadem stole
> And put it in his pocket –
> Queen.　　　　　　　No more.
> [*Enter* Ghost.]　　　　　　(ll. 97–102)

The Ghost enters just as Gertrude is pleading to Hamlet to stop his denunciation. As well as entering at this moment to recall Hamlet from his absorption with Claudius and the Queen, he enters to protect the Queen. He has said before, in his first appearance to Hamlet,

> Taint not thy mind, nor let thy soul contrive
> Against thy mother aught. Leave her to heaven, (I.v. 85–6)

and now he goes on,

> But look, amazement on thy mother sits.
> O, step between her and her fighting soul!
> Conceit in weakest bodies strongest works.
> Speak to her, Hamlet!　　　　　　(III.iv. 113–16)

165

The Ghost is clearly humane rather than vindictive towards Gertrude here. This I think is also an explanation of why he does not appear to her: his appearance would terrify her too much and perhaps turn her mind. And yet what is the effect of the Ghost's reappearance? One thing it does, as Eleanor Prosser points out, is to convince Gertrude that Hamlet is mad.[16] It is very unclear, though, whether this makes any difference to her subsequent behaviour: whether she tells the King of Hamlet's hints of murder, or whether she does or does not 'let the bloat King tempt you again to bed'. We are just not informed of these things. It is difficult then to see that the Ghost can be meant to be preventing Gertrude's repentance, as Miss Prosser suggests. When the King asks her how Hamlet is, in IV.i, she replies without any suggestion of dissimulation:

> Mad as the sea and wind when both contend
> Which is the mightier.   (ll. 7–8)

We might at least agree that the Ghost's reappearance has detracted from the force of Hamlet's criticism of the Queen, and prevented him from finding out the precise degree of her complicity in the murder. The Ghost's very humanity at this point, his tenderness towards Gertrude, has worked against Hamlet's finding out anything more.

The last references to the Ghost in the play – this scene in Gertrude's closet and (if I am right) the echo of the Ghost in Hamlet's 'Now might I do it' speech – both suggest therefore that the ambiguity of the Ghost is finally complicated rather than clarified.

Its elements of corruption impede Hamlet in the prayer-scene, and its very humanity complicates Hamlet's interview with his mother. It is the combination in the Ghost of human evil, fallibility, tenderness, compassion, self-pity, love, revenge, added to the mystery of its supernatural return, that fills Hamlet with a host of conflicting impulses and intensifies the precise contradictions of Hamlet's own nature, the contradictions (between obsession and moral insight) that we have already discussed in this scene.

One might also add that in general Hamlet has deteriorated rather than improved after convincing himself that the Ghost is 'honest': there is his callousness on discovering the body of Polonius, and, at the end of the scene, 'I'll lug the guts into the neighbour room.' There is the elated wit of IV.iii, where he jokes of worms and maggots: we may relish the wit but only if we entirely yield, as it were, to Hamlet's 'charisma' and take a holiday from moral feelings. Hamlet, it seems, is morally destroying himself, and it would be difficult to see beyond the evil inherent in that, at this point.

VI

Before looking at the end of the play we need to examine something of those parts of the play which do not include Hamlet. There is something unsatisfactory in having to take out 'characters' for inspection, and I shall try to avoid that as much as possible. But while trying to preserve a sense of dramatic context, something needs to be said of Claudius, Polonius and the court in general. What kind of perspective on Hamlet, or on the main issues of the play as I have been attempting to explore them, do these other characters and scenes create? Is there any alternative, for the audience's perception of Hamlet, to that which he gives us himself? I have already examined Professor Robson's idea of an alternative perspective in the Play-scene. Are there any other perspectives on the rest of the play?

In i.iii we are transported from the court, and Hamlet's conversation with Horatio, Barnardo and Marcellus about the Ghost, to a very ordinary domestic scene. It is quite new material, and in itself seems to have no bearing as yet on what we have already seen. It is a common practice with Shakespeare to take us to another group of characters and develop them before bringing them into the line of the main plot. But is the burden of this scene merely to give some dimension to Laertes, Polonius, and Ophelia, and to introduce the idea of Hamlet's possible love for Ophelia, or is it supposed to prompt more thought than that? Indeed, what part does Hamlet's relation to Ophelia have in the play as a whole?

The scene soon introduces us to this element with Laertes's speech warning Ophelia about Hamlet. Where do our sympathies lie at this point? The romantic reading would say that since we know Hamlet to be honourable and noble we find Laertes's warnings misplaced, or even offensive. But I would suggest there is a virtue in remaining more neutral at this point. We have seen Hamlet behaving very strangely in the second scene. Particularly we have seen his violent reaction against his mother's remarriage, and his weariness and contempt of his own flesh. These are enough grounds at least to wonder about the nature of his relations with Ophelia. Ophelia later says to Polonius that Hamlet has 'importuned me with love in honourable fashion'. Polonius of course pooh-poohs this. We may naturally tend to take sides against Polonius, who is clearly taking a cynical view: he does not even entertain the possibility of Hamlet's sincerity. But this tendency on our part is not tantamount to saying that we *know* anything about Hamlet's love for Ophelia.

In II.i we see Polonius sending Reynaldo off to spy on Laertes. This episode, which takes up some seventy lines, might seem to be particularly gratuitous, in that it tells us nothing important about the main characters of the play and does not further the plot. But it does have significances for our sense of Polonius and for the moral atmosphere of the play. It shows us Polonius's delight in spyings and stratagems which are to be so instrumental in forwarding the action of the play, and lead in the end to his death behind the arras. It is also notably about sex; Reynaldo is particularly to find out about Laertes's sexual behaviour. This confirms our sense of Polonius's rather prurient inquisitiveness. It also gives another instance of an area of life which has been growing in weight in our sense of the play, the area of sexuality. It is here, notoriously, that moral attitudes are most complex, and moral questions most difficult to settle: an area where the question of perception is likely to be most difficult. In questioning Ophelia or in sending Reynaldo to spy on Laertes, Polonius is demonstrating an inquisitive and overbearing paternal curiosity and exercise of paternal authority. In a very commonplace way, he is an example of parental intrusion into sexual matters. With Ophelia it leads to disaster.

Polonius is a meddling father. The Ghost could not, perhaps, be called just that, since it is not meddling in Hamlet's affairs, but seeking to involve him in its own. But the area of involvement is the same. Would it be too much to say that the play raises questions about sexuality and family relations, and that the Ghost's vengeful insistence on involving Hamlet in its own sexual wrong is not so utterly different from Polonius's jealousy of Ophelia and his spying on his son? So seen, the play would then be partly about the snares of authority in sexual matters. The Ghost's command to Hamlet to avenge his sexual wrong (as well as murder, perhaps even more emphatically than murder) initiates one half of the plot, and Polonius's inquisitiveness and his theories about Hamlet's relations with Ophelia initiate the other: one sets Hamlet to work, in the end, with the Mousetrap; and the other leads to Polonius's death, Ophelia's madness and death, and the King's determination to act against Hamlet, which leads to the climax of the play in the duel.

I am aware that this makes the play sound too schematic, and I am not sure that it would be right to conceive of Shakespeare constructing the play in this way. But there do seem to be some connections here. We do in Polonius see another kind of father whose exercise of paternal authority and whose wrong perception of events has disastrous results. His solicitude for Ophelia is bound up with paternal jealousy, though even more perhaps with his zest for political plotting: but either way there is a lack of concern for Ophelia's individual self and needs. He uses his daughter as a tool. But then the Ghost uses Hamlet as a tool.

How we see Hamlet depends also a great deal on how we see Claudius and Gertrude. We know Hamlet's view of the former: a 'satyr', a 'mildewed ear / Blasting his wholesome brother', a 'treacherous, lecherous, kindless villain', 'a cutpurse of the empire and the rule', 'a thing of shreds and patches', a 'bloat King'. But can we see the King apart from these descriptions? There is no evidence that he is excessively sensual or a drunkard: the stage convention (which in most recent productions of the play seems to have rightly fallen into disuse) that he is to be seen always with a goblet in his hand has almost no foundation in the text. Hamlet says that heavy drinking has always been a custom of the Danes (so that presumably old Hamlet shared the habit?). Claudius's love for Gertrude seems genuine. One of his reasons to Laertes why he has not proceeded against Hamlet after the death of Polonius is that

> The Queen his mother
> Lives almost by his looks, and for myself –
> My virtue or my plague, be it either which –
> She is so conjunctive to my life and soul,
> That, as the star moves not but in his sphere,
> I could not but by her.   (IV.vii. 11–16)

Claudius is, of course, a murderer (which might be borne in mind by one or two of his more ardent supporters, like Wilson Knight). But this does not by itself determine how we respond to him. When we see him at prayer, trying but unable to repent, we may remember Wilson Knight's question: Who in this scene is the better Christian, Hamlet or Claudius? And there is also a way in which Claudius's authoritativeness, courage and directness offset Hamlet's uncertainty, hesitation and obscurity. Claudius is kingly, whereas Hamlet is not (though that is not of course a moral judgement).

Claudius is kingly, but there is enough in the play to suggest that this kingliness is merely a kind of role. Claudius derives strength from his sense of the automatic authority of the king. When Laertes bursts in on him he says:

> Let him go, Gertrude. Do not fear our person.
> There's such divinity doth hedge a king
> That treason can but peep to what it would,
> Acts little of his will. (IV.v. 122–5)

There is of course a brazenness here, in the light of how Claudius attained the throne. But still there seems to be a kind of drawing of strength from the idea of being king. Claudius is, from one point of view, another Player King: a 'thing of shreds and patches', as Hamlet calls him, referring to the motley of the 'Vice' or clown (Dover Wilson's note on the passage). Claudius is an example of a spurious kind of authority, who has the persuasiveness and physical courage of the ruler, but who is morally empty. He has taken on a role in a way which Hamlet hesitates or is unable to do. When in the graveyard Hamlet steps forward amid the mourners at Ophelia's funeral and says 'This is I, Hamlet the Dane', he too is assuming the role of king and the mantle of his father, but it is a histrionic gesture which can have no lasting significance (indeed it is immediately belied by his hysterical wrestling match with Laertes).

In Claudius too, therefore, we see the connected issues of authority and identity in a different way. Claudius assumes authority and gains a kind of working identity, but we see its hollowness. His efficient ability to command is a kind of bluff. He is dedicated simply to bolstering his political power, and to escaping self-knowledge by false consolations: 'All may yet be well.'

Perception, authority, and identity: a reading

This picture of Claudius is too much of a 'character sketch' but its elements are, I think, there in the play. With Gertrude, very much less comes into focus. But it is worth mentioning one or two points: she never reveals that she knew, or did not know, of Claudius's murder of old Hamlet. It is, incidentally, curious that although the Ghost calls Gertrude 'adulterous', and Hamlet repeats the charge, there is no mention in the Mousetrap of the Queen's infidelity to her husband *before* his death. Did Hamlet miss this out because he was uncertain about it, or did he forget to put it in? It is another point, although a tenuous one, at which we may feel that we have slightly conflicting evidence about the nature of Gertrude's infidelity. Again, when she says of Hamlet after Polonius's death, ''A weeps for what is done', it conflicts with the callousness that we have just seen. Is Gertrude sentimentalizing? Or is the discrepancy a small error of focus?

And what of the poetic nature of some of Gertrude's speeches, which seem out of keeping with the morally somnolent figure that constitutes our main impression of Gertrude – the soliloquy describing Ophelia's death, or the picturesque but out-of-place lines on Hamlet's madness in the graveyard?

> This is mere madness;
> And thus awhile the fit will work on him.
> Anon as patient as the female dove
> When that her golden couplets are disclosed,
> His silence will sit drooping.   (v.i. 286–90)

There is an impression of a lack of focus on the character, which could, I think, be seen as part of the whole characteristic difficulty and indeed subject of the play. How do we perceive others? What constitutes their individual identity? How can we act justly towards them? How do we judge? Sometimes, as here with Gertrude, it is a *symptom* of the difficulty as experienced by the playwright himself. A great deal of the rest of the time it is the successfully realized subject of the play.

One character who might have been expected to give us some kind of 'normative' perspective on these questions is Horatio. At the beginning of the play he is presented as something of an authority. The soldiers look to him, as a scholar, to verify the nature of the

171

Ghost. But even Horatio is harrowed with fear and wonder at the apparition, and is unable to explain it. Throughout the rest of the play he is intermittently the companion of Hamlet, but it is difficult to be sure of his assessment of events and even of how much Hamlet tells him. Hamlet admires him because he is not 'passion's slave', and seems to have just those qualities of calm awareness that Hamlet lacks. He might have been made into a kind of choric figure who would provide us with our bearings, but he is not. He remains shadowy, neither fully condoning Hamlet's actions, nor explicitly criticizing them. The stoical elements in him seem ill-equipped to comprehend the forces and problems that Hamlet is exposed to; and his Christianity emerges just enough to agree with Hamlet's pious remark about the 'divinity that shapes our ends' and to feel uneasy about the deaths of Rosencrantz and Guildenstern, but not enough to provide any firm commentary on Hamlet's actions. His final epitaph for Hamlet seems therefore to come from his character as a friend, but not necessarily to have the whole weight of the play behind it.

Like other characters in the play, therefore, Horatio seems to give us glimpses of a critical or at least an 'outside' view of Hamlet, but never decisively enough for us to be sure that this is the central one. We must now turn to the last two acts to see if the play shapes itself into any final 'view'.

VII

'The only justice', wrote D. H. Lawrence, 'is to follow the sincere intuition of the soul, angry or gentle.' The dictum may suggest, I think, a way of seeing the inaction of Hamlet. His struggle throughout the play is to find out in himself 'the sincere intuition of the soul', and the progress of the play as I have been tracing it suggests that he never does discover this intuition. Up to the moment of the Play-scene he sought it by trying to assure himself of the honesty of the Ghost (and to a lesser degree the honesty of Ophelia). But although after the Mousetrap he claims he is certain of the former, his other remarks and the general tenor of his behaviour suggest that this certainty is in fact very qualified, and that he has in no way received the inner assurance which would lead to some kind of decisive action. His perception of good and evil is still blurred, as

172

are his perception of the authority of the Ghost and of his own nature. After the reappearance of the Ghost in the closet-scene Hamlet seems to forget about it. He focuses more fully on himself, perhaps too fully. He is searching for some kind of ground of action and some kind of identity. He does, in fact, have moments at which he finds himself able to act, and it is notable that they are moments at which he is acting simply for himself, and not in pursuance of his 'dread command'. He finds, I suggest, a kind of decisiveness in egoistic action; but it solves none of the essential questions.

The effect of the Play-scene is to provoke Claudius to make a move against Hamlet: Hamlet has in a sense got round the problem of action by getting others to act upon him. At the end of the closet-scene he refers to letters that are to accompany him to England, and speaks with delight of the way he will foil Rosencrantz and Guildenstern, 'will delve one yard below their mines/And blow them at the moon'. When the King turns directly against him he can begin to act, though still not against the King but against the immediate agents of danger to himself. One kind of 'self' Hamlet does not lack, which is why Madariaga's view of Hamlet's egoism is so telling. When it is a matter of his own pride or safety he is decisive enough. But the deeper kind of 'self' – which perhaps should not be called self at all, that real self which I have been calling identity, and Kafka posited as the possible end of genuine self-knowledge and self-denial – this Hamlet cannot discover, perhaps because it is not open to the discoveries of introspection.

For still, in Act IV, Hamlet is above all preoccupied with analysing himself. This is not to say with Coleridge that this introspection is the *cause* of Hamlet's dilemma, but it is one symptom of it. In the famous soliloquy of scene iv, 'How all occasions do inform against me', Hamlet expresses his fundamental ignorance of himself. He does not say that his problem is one of 'thinking too precisely on the event': he says he does not know if it is that or 'bestial oblivion'. The argument for an 'oblivious' Hamlet could indeed be put almost as forcibly as one for a Hamlet 'sicklied o'er with the pale cast of thought'. (There is something of the same strain of pre-occupation with moral 'oblivion' here which we find in the slightly later *Measure for Measure*.) But the lines which ring out from the centre of the play are:

173

> I do not know
> Why yet I live to say, 'This thing's to do,'
> Sith I have cause, and will, and strength, and means
> To do't.   (iv.iv. 43–6)

Whatever holds Hamlet from action is hidden from him, and the tragedy, despite Hamlet's habit of self-analysis (or perhaps partly because of it?), is a tragedy of self-ignorance. 'Cause, and will, and strength, and means': but does that exhaust the elements necessary for just action? What is missing is surely some notion of 'authority' or 'justification'. This is not simply a question of morality. One of the surprising things about the play is, in fact, the way the morality of revenge is nowhere commented on directly. Hamlet speaks of 'excitements of his reason' as well as of his 'blood', and says to Horatio. 'Is't not to be damned / To let this canker of our nature come / In further evil?' (referring, presumably, to Claudius). But this is as close as he gets, after the ostensible testing of the Ghost, to speaking about the morality of revenge. If he had raised the question more fully it would certainly have changed the whole nature of the play, and, as John Lawlor suggests, have made it pass from 'tragic intensity' to 'controversial ardour'.[17] Something deeper is troubling Hamlet than this specific ethical question. What his soliloquies, asides, jests, pronouncements continually return to are the questions: What is man's nature? What is my nature? How can one see clearly? And behind these is an unasked question: What is the source of authority? It is this last element that I have suggested is missing in the soliloquy in iv.iv. Cause and will and strength and means are impotent without some sense of ultimate justification. What Madariaga calls Hamlet's inability to 'be' springs I think from this fundamental source, and this is indicated by the play as a whole, by the whole context. Hamlet does not voice the idea directly, precisely because it is the one thing he is turned away from in his preoccupation with the ambiguous authority of the Ghost in the first half of the play and with himself in the second. It is not, of course, that the play is saying that this prevents him from carrying out his duty of killing Claudius. Rather it is saying that the absence of this authority and clear perception leads to Hamlet's inability to become himself, his inability to find the grounds on which he would either execute the King as he is convinced he must, or (though he does not even suggest this possibility) give up the whole undertaking as the command of an evil Ghost and his own guilt. Lawrence says that any other man would have at once either killed the King or left Denmark.[18]

Hamlet cannot act (or refrain from action) with decision, but he can act casually, or impulsively. The morality of the action is often highly questionable. The first case after the Play-scene is the killing of Polonius. There is no indication when he strikes through the arras that he thinks he may be killing the King: he strikes first and *then* says 'Is it the King?' It is almost a casual action and springs from no deep conviction. His lack of remorse after the murder also suggests a mind too taken up with its own thoughts about mother and King to preserve much moral awareness. The second occasion for action is the replacement of the letters to England with his own letter commanding Rosencrantz and Guildenstern to be put to death. The account of this to Horatio in v.ii. is perhaps the place where Hamlet sounds at his most decisive and commanding. T. S. Eliot cites the passage ('Up from my cabin...') as a prime example of Shakespeare's mature verse, and Coleridge in his 'Essay on Method' makes it his main example of a mind exuberant with activity and yet speaking with clarity and cogency.[19] That the verse should be so notable in this way suggests that Shakespeare, inside the mind of his character, was moved at this point to make Hamlet especially decisive. When we reflect on Hamlet's narrative, this may be seen to be especially significant. Firstly, it is of course only a narrative: we do not see Hamlet doing these things, but only hear him telling of them. His delight in the narration may derive in part from his decisiveness in the actions themselves, but it derives partly too from Hamlet's gifts as a talker. He seems so assured here partly because he is *talking* about what has happened, summing it up in comprehensible form. When it comes to the mental martialling of experience Hamlet is in his element. Secondly, the actions he is describing are notable too. Hamlet is here acting solely in self-defence and not against the King. In replacing Claudius's message with his own he is also taking upon himself the authority of king, and in sealing his message with his father's signet he is going further, and assuming the authority of his father.[20] This assumption of independent royal authority accounts, I suggest, for his delight in his action: he is

175

deliberately for the first time acting for himself and acting as king. Yet it is after all a small achievement in relation to his larger problem. His speech is not just to give us details of the plot, but to show how delightedly he talks about and emphasizes this moment of action.

His enthusiasm and conviction may also account for the way he seems surprisingly convinced that God was at this moment on his side, that behind his rashness was 'a divinity that shapes our ends/Rough hew them how we will'; and for his remark about his having his father's signet with him, 'Why even in that was heaven ordinant'. We may doubt the truth of both these convictions when we remember the deaths of the courtiers, who are not shown to be guilty, whatever Hamlet thinks: in any event they clearly did not know of the sealed death-warrant. Hamlet's invocations of God here, and elsewhere too perhaps, are momentary and even casual.

When Hamlet is acting on behalf of himself he can be decisive enough, but when he returns to the matter of the revenge his tone changes. There seems to me something surprising about his exclamation to Horatio at this stage in the action (v.ii). It seems to be casting about for motivation:

> Does it not, think thee, stand me now upon –
> He that hath killed my king, and whored my mother,
> Popped in between th'election and my hopes,
> Thrown out his angle for my proper life,
> And with such coz'nage – is't not perfect conscience
> To quit him with this arm? And is't not to be damned
> To let this canker of our nature come
> In further evil? (ll. 63–70)

After his saying in Act IV that he has 'cause, and will, and strength, and means' to kill the King, it is strange that Hamlet should still be seeking reassurance, as if he is still not convinced in some way. But the element he adds which was not in the soliloquy is the element of 'conscience': and he is appealing to Horatio as a kind of independent authority. Yet the piling on of reasons – making his own thwarted ambition an equal motive with his father's murder and his mother's possible adultery, and then throwing in Claudius's trickery as another motive – weakens the force of the appeal even while trying to strengthen it. The question is of course largely rhetorical, and Horatio does not reply: but in his silence may one

176

not also see a faint glimmer of uncertainty? Horatio seems again very quiet in this scene. His 'Why that's most certain' in reply to Hamlet's remark about divinity seems merely a pious conventional assent; and 'So Rosencrantz and Guildenstern go to it' carries more than a hint of censure.

How we see Hamlet on his return from England is crucial to how we feel about the end of the play and indeed about the tragedy as a whole. Those critics who feel that Hamlet dies carrying out a 'sacred duty' tend to argue that Hamlet is a changed man, that his doubts have disappeared, and that he has achieved a mood of religious acceptance. But it is difficult to follow what Hamlet says and does with quite this certainty. It is difficult to see a Christian significance in the graveyard-scene (as, say, Eleanor Prosser does) when Hamlet concentrates so exclusively on the mere physical facts of death, and gives no hint that he entertains any ideas of an afterlife, Christian or other. It is also difficult to feel that Hamlet's outburst at Ophelia's grave is a show of genuine love and grief. Hamlet has killed Ophelia's father and is therefore indirectly responsible for her madness and death. Would not true feeling have been mixed with remorse here, and have led to something other than this rowdy battle of words with Laertes?

In any event there seems to be something melodramatic, not to say irreverent, in Hamlet's self-announcement: 'This is I, Hamlet the Dane' ['Don't pay so much attention to Ophelia and Laertes; *I* have arrived']. If Hamlet were about to reveal everything, and act, the feeling of the speech might be different. But as it is there are two things to notice about the speech: firstly, Hamlet is pretending to assume kingly authority by using the title of the king (as Dover Wilson points out). He is making as if to assert his identity by asserting his role as the ultimate authority in the state. One might be reminded here (as earlier in Hamlet's use of his father's signet, the Danish seal) of Lawrence's idea that Hamlet has to decide 'To be or not to be King, Father, in the self, supreme', and feel that for a brief moment he has decided 'to be'. But at the same time the announcement has something puerile about it: it comes from the egoistic surface rather than from the depths of the self. Hamlet, one might suggest, needs to find a deeper sense of authority than can come by simply pretending to be king.

If the reader follows me in this he will agree that the resigned,

177

chastened and religious Hamlet of many critics dwindles considerably. But what then are we to make of the most powerful single piece of evidence for this view, Hamlet's speech about Providence in v.ii, after Osric has invited him to the fencing match? Here, it is argued, Hamlet finally expresses his sense of a higher authority, and commits himself to God. 'You will lose this wager my lord', says Horatio; and Hamlet:

> I do not think so. Since he went into France I have been in continual practice. I shall win at the odds. But thou wouldst not think how ill all's here about my heart. But it is no matter.
>
> *Horatio.* Nay, good my lord –
> *Hamlet.* It is but foolery, but it is such a kind of gaingiving as would perhaps trouble a woman.
> *Horatio.* If your mind dislike anything, obey it. It will forestall their repair hither and say you are not fit.
> *Hamlet.* Not a whit, we defy augury. There is special providence in the fall of a sparrow. If it be now, 'tis not to come; if it be not to come, it will be now; if it be not now, yet it will come. The readiness is all. Since no man of aught he leaves knows, what is't to leave betimes? Let be. (ll. 211–25)

This is eloquent and moving, but what does it express? An acceptance of death put in specifically Christian terms, certainly; and we may admit here that Hamlet has come to terms with dying, in a sense. But of his so-called 'duty' in the one task which, it is argued, he must accomplish, there is nothing. Bradley himself comments that these lines

seem to express the kind of religious resignation which, however beautiful in one aspect, really deserves the name of fatalism rather than that of faith in Providence. In place of this determination the Hamlet of the Fifth Act shows a kind of sad or indifferent self-abandonment, as if he secretly despaired of forcing himself to action, and were ready to leave his duty to some other power than his own.[21]

Moreover, if Hamlet does not fear the possibility of being killed, and he does not seem to here, what is it that he still seems to dread? Something is troubling him which is not the fear of the duel, and it seems to me that any account of this scene must take the full weight of that powerful line, 'But thou wouldst not think how ill all's here about my heart.' It might be described as I have done in Chapter 7 above, as the Kierkegaardian experience of dread: a dread

178

of the future, of the equal possibility of good and evil, and of being judged.

The last scene of *Hamlet* moves with exciting swiftness. Hamlet enters carelessly on the fencing match, and we feel that events, the mechanism of the King's plot, are in control and sweeping things to their conclusion. (The Russian actor Smoktunovsky, in Kozintsev's film of the play, gave a thrilling portrayal of Hamlet at this point, riding on a wave of events, but detached, almost ironic, as if he were making no final commitment to action or making it in spite of himself.) There is almost the Mallarméan sense of the chance throw of the dice, the abandonment of decision, but perhaps in order to overcome chance by proving its powerlessness. For there is no sense of 'decisive' action from Hamlet, of action, that is, which would decide the issues raised in the play (the honesty of the Ghost, the nature of Hamlet). Hamlet acts impulsively, casually, as he did in killing Polonius; and the final killing of Claudius is done in a spirit of egoism. Madariaga noted the significant point that when Hamlet kills the King it is in the heat of anger at his own death-wound, not in the spirit of finally carrying out justice.[22] Even the feeling of revenge comes only as he seizes the poisoned cup, and, forcing it between the King's lips, cries:

> Here, thou incestuous, murderous, damnèd Dane,
> Drink off this potion. Is thy union here?
> Follow my mother. (v.ii. 326–8)

And here Hamlet's uppermost feeling is his old horror at his mother's remarriage, the old obsession which more than anything else has clouded his mind and impeded his perception and action.

The spectator of this seems to be torn radically between being compelled to relish (or to be horrified by) the full flood of Hamlet's vindictiveness, and following Laertes in his feeling that 'he's justly served.' The feeling here must be ambiguous for there is no final directive for us to follow. Our perspective is still multiple. Horatio and Fortinbras both seem to see their *own* Hamlet, the one a 'noble heart' whom flights of angels shall sing to his rest, and the other the soldier and hero who 'was likely, had be been put on, / To have proved most royal'. The spectator must respond to these tributes,

179

but can they be the whole of one's response? For Horatio speaks too of the bitter and undismissable realities,

> Of carnal, bloody, and unnatural acts,
> Of accidental judgements, casual slaughters,
> Of deaths put on by cunning and forced cause. (ll. 382–4)

Do we have any final and dominant view of Hamlet as the play closes? His very last words are worth noting:

> I cannot live to hear the news from England.
> But I do prophesy th' election lights
> On Fortinbras. He has my dying voice.
> So tell him, with th'occurrents, more and less.
> Which have solicited – the rest is silence.   (ll. 355–9)

He dies having just given two commands; for a brief moment he has been king, and he exercises his kingly authority in giving the throne to Fortinbras. He also commands Horatio to tell his story. The authority which he merely played at before (that of king) he grasps for a second. But the sense of a deeper authority, against which he might have defined himself, has eluded him. It is a tantalizing act for him to pass the task of explanation to Horatio, for what do we imagine Horatio is going to say? There is no final judgement of Hamlet attempted by anyone in the play: Fortinbras talks simply of what might have been.

VIII

Does the play as a whole formulate any kind of judgement on Hamlet and the action? *Hamlet* lacks any clear religious framework, Christian or other. It does not have the clear concern with Christian morality of *Measure for Measure*, or the strongly suggested Christian values implicit in *Macbeth*, or even the varying and conflicting expressions of belief we find in *King Lear*. There are several references to Christian belief, but they do not, I think, amount to any central value in the play, and merely serve to provide a background of conventional doctrine which comments at times on the action but does not provide any final standard. In his first soliloquy Hamlet wishes 'that the Everlasting had not fixed/His canon 'gainst self-slaughter', but the reference may be merely conventional, even cursory, for Hamlet nowhere expresses anxiety over the fact that the Everlasting has also fixed his canon against revenge. In the 'To be...' soliloquy Hamlet seems to have forgotten about this religious prohibition of suicide and refers only to the fears of 'what dreams may come': there is no idea of any Christian afterlife. One need only remind oneself briefly of the distinctly un-Christian feelings Hamlet expresses at various moments (particularly in the nunnery-scene, and when he finds the King at prayer). More problematic is the Christian reference in Act V – Hamlet's observation about Providence – on which many interpretations of the end of the play turn. I have argued that the state of Hamlet's soul is far from clear, though we do register a change of mood; and that one cannot see any commitment here to divine authority, so that Horatio's 'flights of angels' is more a heartfelt wish than any decisive summing-up of our feelings.

The most distinctly Christian moment in the play is Claudius's prayer of attempted repentance, a powerful representation of a Christian conscience struggling unavailingly with itself, and of the idea of the ultimate authority of the Last Judgement:

> There is no shuffling; there the action lies
> In his true nature, and we ourselves compelled,
> Even to the teeth and forehead of our faults,
> To give in evidence. (III.iii. 61–4)

But there is no such judgement for the play as a whole, in which we may see the action 'in his true nature'; and this absence is an essential part of the complexity of the play. For Claudius's evil is unambiguous: he is aware of the exact nature of his crimes in Christian terms, but is too weak morally to reverse the actions and repent. What seems to ensnare Hamlet's thoughts, and those of the play, is a sense of evil of a more complex kind, complicated by the condition of the perceiver and mixed with the springs of action, so that good and evil cannot be untwined from one another.

Hamlet moves in a world in which he finds no final authority. His supposed 'proof' of the Ghost's honesty, is, I have argued, a shallow one; nor does it confirm Hamlet in any course of action. After that, Hamlet's course is one partly of casual and impulsive action and partly of submission to other people's plots, accompanied by his habitual self-scrutiny. 'Cause and will, and strength, and means' to kill the King are not enough, and Hamlet does not identify the missing element of justice, justification or authority. It is as if Hamlet turns away from this after his encounters with the Ghost, the goodness of which he never really proves. The father whom Hamlet habitually compares to a god or the gods has returned in a guise that seems to speak simultaneously of heaven and hell. It may seem to confer a duty, but its nature is flawed by the very corruption it sends Hamlet out to destroy.

But, historically minded critics will say, is this not to commit what might be called a 'universalist' fallacy, and forget that *Hamlet* is a play written in a particular place and at a particular time in which the modern *angst* and the modern Absurd would have been incomprehensible?

There seem to me to be two answers to this. Firstly there is the appeal to the idea that a great work of art is 'great' because in many ways it transcends its time. It grows out of local conditions but it inhabits a world in which it has a timeless life. It becomes a kind of symbol of human nature which is open to the different interpretations of different ages. There is always the object itself which should control our description and interpretation, but beyond that what we bring to it is as important (at least in the process of our perception of it) as what we receive from it. There may be aspects of a great work which are revealed only to successive ages and never become apparent in its own age. And this seems particularly true of *Hamlet*, which seems to lend itself so uniquely to a variety of descriptions, interpretations and evaluations. Dr Johnson saw 'variety' as one of the play's notable attributes, and where there is such variety there must be varieties of emphasis on what is 'central'. I have suggested too that *Hamlet* is about the problems of interpretation: that in every respect it makes us aware of the vagaries of perception, the possibilities of different perspectives, in the way the characters view events and each other, and in turn in the way we view those characters and events. Neither Hamlet nor we discover any one 'right' perspective. It is, in this sense, a tragedy of perspective.

Secondly, I would want to argue that there is enough in the context of the Elizabethan age at least to allow the possibility of such a play at such a time. There is Donne's great 'Satyre III' on the problem of religious doubt and authority, with its sense that in the end religious truth eludes the doctrines of any one perspective: we must be continually seeking the source. Donne wrote of the matter, too, in ways that recall *Hamlet* and the relation between religious authority and paternal authority:

> But unmov'd thou
> Of force must one, and forc'd but one allow;
> And the right; aske thy father which is she,
> Let him aske his. (ll. 69–72)

But more strictly relevant to *Hamlet* is the example of Montaigne.

It was T. S. Eliot who said cryptically that to understand the play we would like to know 'whether, and when, and after or at the same time as what experience Shakespeare read Montaigne II.xii, *Apologie de Raimond Sebond*'.[23] It is an essay which, as Dover Wilson has shown, echoes throughout the play, and seems to provide at times a source for certain of Shakespeare's passages and also a kind of oblique commentary on them. The fundamental idea of the essay is that man is a creature of radically limited vision. His perception cannot hope to solve the problems of the world or his own consciousness and his great need is to turn outward towards a God whom he cannot know but in whom he must have faith. *Hamlet* provides no such doctrine, but it echoes at many points the quiet ironies and sense of absurdity of Montaigne's text. It is as if the play takes from Montaigne his quizzical, sceptical frame of mind, but leaves us in that state of scepticism without suggesting the larger frame of reference.

When we read Montaigne, for instance, we may remember Hamlet's great prose panegyric on the splendours of man and the heavens ('What a piece of work is man'), and his disillusioned sense of his own inability to delight in them:

> ... and indeed, it goes so heavily with my disposition that this goodly frame the earth, seems to me a sterile promontory; this most excellent canopy, the air, look you, this brave o'erhanging firmament, this majestical roof fretted with golden fire: why, it appeareth nothing to me but a foul and pestilent congregation of vapours. (II.ii. 305–11)

Montaigne seems almost to comment on this:

Who hath perswaded [man], that this admirable moving of heavens vaults; that the eternal light of these lampes so fiercely rowling over his head; that the horror-moving and continuall motion of this infinite vast Ocean, were established, and continue so many ages for his commoditie and service?[24]

Hamlet is a humanist whose gaze is inward, or who sees the universe revolving round his individual consciousness. Earth, air and the firmament are to him the 'frame', 'canopy' and 'roof' of man's own dwelling, rather than the 'heavens vaults', the 'eternal light' and the 'horror-moving' motion of Montaigne's skies, stars and ocean. In however large and noble a sense, Hamlet is still the egoist here, whereas Montaigne attempts to see man in a different perspective. Again Hamlet complains, 'O that this too too solid flesh would melt', seeing it as a particular individual condition. For Montaigne the burden of the physical is a given for all men:

Our corruptible body doth overlode our soule, and our dwelling on earth weighes downe our sense that is set to thinke of many matters. (p. 142)

Hamlet is confronted with two commands: 'Revenge his foul and most unnatural murder', and 'Remember me.' They are the primal commandments that dominate the world of the play in all their moral ambiguity. Montaigne tells us:

The first law that ever God gave unto man, was a Law of pure obedience
(p. 186)

The claim on Hamlet's obedience is powerful and fills the vision of the play in a way that blots out the deeper claim of obedience to God. Coming from a Ghost, and the Ghost of a man Hamlet almost deified, the claim seems indeed almost to replace the profounder one, in a kind of 'false transcendence'. Hamlet's father was for him a kind of god, a Hyperion, Mars, Mercury, Jove himself. Man himself is 'in action how like an angel, in apprehension how like a god'. But Montaigne spoke of

that fond title which *Aristotle* gives us of mortal gods, and that rash judgement of *Chrysippus*, that *Dion* was virtuous as a God. (p. 188)

Elsewhere in the same essay Montaigne writes:

Superstition obaieth pride as a father, (p. 199)

184

which, if one applies it to *Hamlet*, makes one wonder whether Hamlet's obedience to the Ghost might not indeed be superstition obeying pride. Hamlet's constant introspection, his speculations about death, the drifting arguments of the 'To be...' soliloquy, receive a commentary in Montaigne's

Mans minde could never be maintained, if it were still floting up and downe in this infinite deepe of shapeless conceits.   (p. 217)

And when Horatio remarks on Hamlet's tracing the body of Alexander until he found it stopping a bunghole,

'Twere to consider too curiously to consider so,   (v.i. 207–8)

he might have been recalling Montaigne's very words (in Florio):

Keepe your selves in the common path, it is not good to be so subtill, and so curious.   (p. 271)

If we think of Montaigne's essay we can find an adequate point of reference for the play in its own period, which gives a kind of historical grounding for some of the questions I have been discussing: the fallibility of man's perception, his lack of self-knowledge, and his need for the experience of authority.

But I would prefer to end by returning to a comparison closer to our own time, in the spirit of my general idea that by being alive to the predominant concerns of modern writers we can gain insight into elements of Shakespeare's play which are 'there', but of which we can be more fully conscious than were previous ages (just as there are doubtless aspects of the play which are less available to us). The comparison is with the great religious artist of our own time, Franz Kafka. Kafka's is a world, as I have suggested above, in which the manifestations of authority are always ambiguous, and the perceptions of the protagonist are always limited. The sense of ultimate value is always uncertain but never entirely disappears. Authority is morally compelling, tyrannical, grotesque, solicitous, awe-inspiring, pitiable, comic and absurd. Men's perspective on it is always distorted. A father condemns his son to death for attempting to marry; a man turns into an insect and is in turn tended, avoided and finally destroyed by his family; a bank clerk is arrested by a shadowy court that is an infinite recession of chaotic authorities, and which finally sends two 'waterflies' to lead him to his execution; a land surveyor never discovers the authority in the castle which employs him, and is helped (or hindered?) by two indistinguishable assistants.

The world in which a man is given the command to revenge by his father's ghost, in which he sees himself 'crawling between earth and heaven', and in which he is attended by a Rosencrantz and a Guildenstern and summoned to his death by an Osric, does not seem so very far from this. The revelation from another world which gives Hamlet his task or burden is radically ambiguous, and the evil it reveals is inseparable from an evil in which it seems to share. Because he cannot perceive authority, either outside or within himself, or discover a genuine instinct for right action, Hamlet cannot 'maintain his mind' or achieve a firm sense of identity. In the last speech of the play Fortinbras says:

> Bear Hamlet like a soldier to the stage,
> For he was likely, had he been put on,
> To have proved most royal.

As I have suggested, it might seem a supreme irony: whoever was 'put on' so much as Hamlet? But perhaps it has a hidden truth. Hamlet has never come to the point of decisive action and self-realization. Tolstoy may have been right to say that Hamlet has 'no character'; but it may be a subject of the play rather than a fault.[25] In a play of such stature and complexity it is, notoriously, difficult to distinguish between the ambiguities and limitations of the central character and those of the art by which he is presented. But there remains something indeterminate and unrealized about Hamlet, and about the play as a whole; and it is this indeterminacy, combined with such rich human suggestiveness, that has caused the ghosts of the play to reappear so often in the pages of modern literature, as if in search of the interpretation and definition which the play itself does not provide.

Notes

Introduction

1 One of 'Zhivago's Poems' in *Doctor Zhivago*, translated by Max and Manya Harari (London, 1958). Henry Gifford, in his *Pasternak* (Cambridge, 1977), notes that what impressed Pasternak about *Hamlet* was 'the spirit of sacrifice'. In Pasternak's *Notes to Translations of Shakespeare's Tragedies*, Gifford comments, there is nothing comparable in his view to that of Eliot or Lawrence. 'Pasternak sees only the heroism of a born prince who had a destiny to fulfil in the service of times after his own' (p. 153).
2 In *Poems of Akhmatova*, selected, translated and introduced by Stanley Kunitz and Max Hayward (London, 1974).
3 W. B. Yeats, *Autobiographies* (London, 1961), p. 47.
4 'Hamlet Once More', *Philistinism in England and America*, ed. R. H. Super, (Ann Arbor, 1974), p. 191.

Chapter 1

1 Quoted in *Œuvres Complètes*, ed. Henri Mondor and G. Jean-Aubry (Paris, 1945), p. 1564. Quotations from Mallarmé are from this edition. My general practice in this and the next two chapters has been to translate passages of prose, but to leave verse in the text in the original; I have provided my own translations of many of the verse passages in the notes below. I have not attempted to render the quality of the verse but merely to provide a simple and literal prose version.
2 Baudelaire, *Œuvres Complètes* (Paris, 1961), pp. 110–11. Translation: 'Let us contemplate at leisure this caricature / And this shadow of Hamlet imitating his posture, / His indecisive look and his hair in the wind. / Isn't it a great shame to see this good chap, / This tramp, this actor on holiday, this clown, / Because he knows how to play his role artistically, / Wanting to interest with his song of sorrows / The eagles, the crickets, the streams and the flowers / And even to us, authors of these old items, / To recite howling his public tirades?'
 This satirical use of the image of Hamlet for the failed poet is partly echoed in an early version of Mallarmé's poem 'Le Guignon' (The Jinx),

187

which is however a much more bitter and desperate rendering of the theme. The poet, who has Promethean ambitions (but no vulture), is dogged by the Jinx and left an old beggar, the butt of urchins, whores and ragamuffins. The early version ends:

Quand chacun a sur eux craché tous les dédains,
Nus, assoiffés de grand, et priant le tonnerre,
Ces Hamlet abreuvés de malaises badins

Vont ridiculement se pendre au réverbère.

The image is interesting in the way it shows Mallarmé's association of Hamlet with the ambiguous idealism and absurdity of the poet, an association that is again present in 'Le Pitre Châtié'.

3 For a discussion of various comparisons see Helen Bailey, *Hamlet in France* (Geneva, 1964), pp. 138ff. I am indebted to Miss Bailey for several references in the present and the following chapter; also to T. J. B. Spencer's 'The Decline of Hamlet', *Stratford-On-Avon Studies*, vol. 5, ed. J. R. Brown and B. Harris (London, 1963).

4 Baudelaire, *Œuvres Complètes*, p. 971.

5 Translation: 'Eyes, lakes with my simple drunkenness to be reborn / Other than the actor who with a gesture evoked / As with a pen the ignoble soot of the gas-lamps, / I have made a window in the wall of cloth. / A limpid treacherous swimmer with my leg and arms, / With multiplied bounds, denying the evil / Hamlet! It is as if in the wave I was introducing / A thousand tombs in order to disappear into them virgin. / Hilarious gold of a cymbal beaten by fists, / Suddenly the sun strikes the nudity / Which breathes itself pure from my mother-of-pearl freshness, / Rancid night of the skin when you were passing over me, / Not knowing, ungrateful as I was, that it was my whole anointing, / This greasepaint drowned in the perfidious water of the glaciers.'

6 Wallace Fowlie, *Mallarmé* (London, 1953), p. 94. I am also indebted to Mr Fowlie's book in my subsequent discussion of *Igitur* and 'Un Coup de Dés'.

7 See René Taupin, 'The Myth of Hamlet in France in Mallarmé's Generation', *Modern Language Quarterly*, XIV, 4, p. 433.

8 See J. P. Richard, *L'univers imaginaire de Mallarmé* (Paris, 1961), pp. 443–6.

9 Published in *La Revue Blanche*, July 1896. Quoted in *Œuvres Complètes*, p. 1564.

10 Unless otherwise indicated, quotations from *Hamlet* throughout my text are taken from the New American Library edition, ed. Edward Hubler (New York and London, 1963).

11 Claudel, *Œuvres Complètes* (Paris, 1959). First published in the *Nouvelle Revue Française*, numéro d'hommage à Stéphane Mallarmé, 1 Nov.

1926. Dr Bonniot, in Mallarmé's *Œuvres Complètes*, also describes Igitur as 'a kind of more impersonal Hamlet' (p. 427).

12 See Bailey, *Hamlet in France*, p. 140. We also know from other sources that around 1875–6, the time of his reported conversation with Moore, Mallarmé was contemplating a substantial new dramatic project, a 'grand travail', a 'drame magique, populaire et lyrique', a 'théâtre entièrement nouveau'. There is some reason to associate this with the Hamlet play Moore speaks of, and hence with the earlier *Igitur* of 1869 (see H. M. Block, *Mallarmé and the Symbolist Drama* (Connecticut, 1977), pp. 49–50). The projected play sounds as if it would have been quite different from the esoteric drama of the mind, *Igitur*. It is interesting that Mallarmé seems to have been contemplating both kinds of play at the same time: Shakespeare, of course, combined precisely these two kinds of play in *Hamlet*. It is also interesting that Mallarmé owned one of Manet's illustrations of *Hamlet* and displayed it on the wall of his apartment: it depicted Hamlet 'with drawn sword, in a very theatrical pose, his back turned to his friends, gazing out into empty space' (see Taupin, 'The Myth of Hamlet in France', p. 438). This picture of Hamlet gazing into the void – or is it at the Ghost? – seems suggestive in relation to Mallarmé's drama, in *Igitur*, of a confrontation with 'le néant'.

13 Translation: 'The solid tomb where lies all that is harmful, / And the miserly silence and the massive night'.

14 Translation: 'Myself, solicitous of your wishes, I wish to see, / For him who vanished, yesterday, in the ideal / Duty which the gardens of this star make for us, / Survive for the honour of the tranquil disaster / A solemn agitation in the air / Of words, drunken purple and great clear calyx, / Which, rain and diamond, the diaphanous glance / Fallen there on the flowers of which none there fade, / Isolates amid the hour and the sunbeam of the day.' (Instead of the Pléiade edition's 'reste' I have taken an alternative reading of 'resté' for the penultimate line here.)

15 Quoted in Mallarmé, *Œuvres Complètes*, p. 1580.

16 The question of the order of composition of the plays is, of course, a difficult if not impossible one, since the hard evidence of records of performance, entries in the Stationers' Register and publication, and the less determinate evidence of stylistic factors, are not enough to provide grounds for certainty. I follow what seems to be the current scholarly consensus in dating the composition of *Hamlet* in 1601–2, closely preceded by *Twelfth Night* and *Julius Caesar*, and followed by *Troilus and Cressida* (1602–3). As T. S. Eliot points out, *Hamlet* has elements of Shakespeare's earliest and his most developed styles. At any rate, it is clear that it is the first of what we now see as the great tragedies, and I think one can fairly regard it, coming where it does, as a kind of watershed in the progress of his drama, which unites the

elements from many different tributaries; from the romantic language of *Romeo and Juliet*, the historical perspective and the tragic apprehensions of Brutus in *Julius Caesar*, the songs and the darker parts of the comedy of *Twelfth Night*, and the bitter analytic spirit which was to find expression in *Troilus and Cressida*. In remarking on the premonition of *Hamlet* in the fight between Romeo and Paris in Juliet's tomb, Stevie Smith has used the metaphor in the title of the present study in a different sense: 'Are not all Shakespeare's plays really versions, schemes and ghosts of *Hamlet?*' (*Novel On Yellow Paper* (London, 1969), p. 202).

17 In Mallarmé, *Œuvres Complètes*, p. 299.

18 Translation: 'A plume solitary bewildered / Unless a cap of midnight meets it or touches it lightly / and immobilizes / in velvet crumpled by a dark burst of laughter / this rigid whiteness / ridiculous / in opposition to the sky / too much not to distinguish / minutely / whoever / bitter prince of the reef / dresses his head with it as with the heroical / irresistible / but contained / by his small virile reason / in thunder / anxious / expiatory and pubescent'.

19 Translation: 'Plummets / the plume / rhythmic suspense of the sinister / to bury itself / in the original foam'.

Chapter 2

1 W. W. Robson, 'Did the King See the Dumb-Show?', *Cambridge Quarterly*, VI, 4 (1975).

2 Translated from Claudel, *Œuvres Complètes*, vol. XV, p. 113.

3 Valéry, *Œuvres Complètes*, vol. I (Paris, 1957), pp. 988–1014.

Chapter 3

1 Quotations from Laforgue's poetry are taken from the Livre de Poche edition (Paris, 1970); p. 323. Translation: 'All will perish! Your hands which held the reins / In the wood in such a noble fashion, / Your stomach, skin flaccid and creasing into wrinkles / Your finch's brains, / Your sugared intestines / Your supple dancing-girl's feet, / Your pink palms, your heart, / And your clitoris which you twisted swooning / In long spasms of langour.'

2 Michael Collie, *Laforgue* (Edinburgh and London, 1963), p. 16.

3 Translation: 'The woman screams at night, twists herself and bites the sheets / To bring forth vile, unhappy, ungrateful children. / Half of them die within a year, in misery, / Without counting the stillborn fit to hide under the earth. / Man, flowers, nests, all labour in vain, / For life is every hour a bitter battle.'

4 Translation: 'To the Good Knight-Errant, / Restaurant, / Furnished hotel, reading rooms, current prices'.

5 Collie, *Laforgue*, Ch. III.
6 *Moralités Légendaires* is to be found in vol. III of Laforgue's *Œuvres Complètes* (Paris, 1924).
7 The number of 22 October 1886.
8 Translation: 'Twilight comes; the little port / Lights its fires. / Ah! the familiar decor! / The rain continues to dampen the river, / The sky weeps pointlessly, without anything moving it.'
9 Translation: 'The nasal bells of Sundays / Abroad / Cause what there is of the enraged cow in me.'
10 Translation: 'With what pleasure would I wring / Your heart, your body.'
11 Translation: 'Briefly, I was going to deliver myself of an "I love you" / When, I realized not without pain / That first of all I was not fully in possession of myself.'
12 Translation: 'And it's not just her flesh which would be everything to me / And I wouldn't just be just a great heart for her, / But what are madmen going to do / In fraternal stories! / Spirit and flesh, flesh and spirit, / It is the noble and edenic spirit / To be a Man a little with a Woman.'
13 Translation: '– Let's go, last of the poets, / Always shut up like this you'll drive yourself mad! / Look, it's fine, everyone's out of doors, / So go and buy yourself two penn'orth of hellebore, / That'll give you a little walk.'
14 Translation: 'There, there, I shall make you ashamed! / And I shall bring you to book for that corset bending your back, for your bustle and curled hair / perversely stacking up your forehead and hind-quarters.'
15 Translation: 'Her rainy boudoirs bathe in blood / My useless adolescent heart.../ And I fell asleep. At dawn I fled.../ It's all the same to me today.'
16 Translation: '(Voracious eyes keen on the quarry; / A mouth forever intimate!) / (– See how she honours me with her confidences; / I suffer from them more than she thinks!)'
17 Translation: 'Yesterday the orchestra attacked / Its last polka.'
18 Translation: 'Go, your least winks are perjuries. / Be quiet, with you types nothing lasts. / Be quiet, be quiet. / One loves but once.'
19 Translation: 'It's the sweetness of legends, of the age of gold, / Of the legends of Antigones, / Sweetness which makes one ask: / So when did all that happen? /...Isn't there plenty there to bleed?/ To bleed? Me, kneaded up from the purest mud of Cybele! / Me, who might have been to her in all the art of the Adams / Of the Edens as hyperbolically faithful / As the Sun is every evening towards the Occident'.
20 Translation: '(Oh! How thin she's grown! / What will become of her?/ Soften, soften,/ You, clots of memory!)'

191

Chapter 4

1 From 'The Love Song of J. Alfred Prufrock'. Quotations from Eliot's poems are taken from *The Complete Poems and Plays, 1909–1950* (New York, 1952).
2 Salvador de Madariaga, *On Hamlet* (New York, 1964), p. 95.
3 'Hamlet and his Problems', in *The Sacred Wood* (London, 1919); reprinted in Eliot's *Selected Essays* (London, 1966) as 'Hamlet'.
4 Published in *The Criterion*, III, 10 (Jan. 1925), pp. 278–81.
5 See F. O. Matthiessen, *The Achievement of T. S. Eliot*, 3rd edn (New York and London, 1958), p. 73.

Chapter 5

1 London, 1972; London, 1959.
2 London, 1977.
3 Edmund Wilson, *Axel's Castle* (Glasgow, 1976), Ch. 6 (e.g. p. 172).
4 *Ulysses*, Bodley Head edn (London, 1967), p. 274. Subsequent quotations are from this edition.
5 Joyce's simple and moving poem 'Ecce Puer', written on his son's birthday in 1932 and shortly after the death of his father, suggests the abiding memory of *his* alienation, and also a spirit of forgiveness which bequeaths 'love and mercy' to the child. Might one not contrast this to the spirit of revenge which old Hamlet bequeaths to his son; a bequest which in turn, in his eccentric biographical theory of *Hamlet*, Joyce has Shakespeare making to his son, Hamnet? The connection tells us little about Shakespeare but a lot about Joyce. The poem ends:

> A child is sleeping;
> An old man gone.
> O, father, foresaken,
> Forgive your son!

6 Hélène Cixous, *The Exile of James Joyce*, English edn (London, 1976), p. 564. Miss Cixous has a complex account of the role *Hamlet* played in Joyce's imagination. It is occasionally suggestive, but her over-all view is mingled with many other threads of argument and I find it often obscure. Essentially she seems to propose an idea of Stephen's identification with Shakespeare and Shakespeare's with the Ghost. She does not consider the idea that Bloom's sense of *Hamlet* is also important, or that Stephen has to escape the notion of the vengeful artist which his theory of *Hamlet* involves. I have also found useful in this connection Weldon Thornton's *Allusions in 'Ulysses': An Annotated List* (Chapel Hill, 1968).
　　Esau was also a usurped brother, and seems, like some of the phrases preceding his mention in the quote from Joyce ('Speech, speech... Lapwing', p. 61), to have further associations with the *Hamlet* theme.

Chapter 6

1 *Collected Poems* (London, 1967), p. 494.
2 In 'The Novel', in *Phoenix II (Uncollected and Unpublished and Other Prose Works)*, ed. W. Roberts and H. T. Moore (London, 1968), p. 417.
3 Reprinted in *Phoenix (The Posthumous Papers of D. H. Lawrence)* (London, 1967), p. 439.
4 *Twilight in Italy*, Penguin edition (Harmondsworth, 1960), p. 70.
5 Reprinted in *Phoenix*, pp. 223–31.
6 Reprinted in *ibid.* pp. 551–84.
7 Quotations from *Women in Love* are taken from the Penguin edition (Harmondsworth, 1963).
8 Book I of the *Memoirs of Eleanor Farjeon* (London, 1958), p. 136.
9 Reprinted in *Phoenix*, pp. 587–665. This quotation, pp. 621–2.

Chapter 7

1 Søren Kierkegaard, *Stages on Life's Way*, trans. Walter Lowrie (Princeton, 1940), pp. 409–11.
2 In *The Anchor Review* (New York, 1955), pp. 109–27, reprinted in *Love Declared* (Boston, 1961). I am indebted to this essay for drawing my attention to Kierkegaard's appendix on Hamlet, discussed above.
3 *The Concept of Dread*, trans. Walter Lowrie (Princeton, 1957); Translator's Preface, p. x.
4 *The Journals of Søren Kierkegaard*, ed. and trans. Alexander Dru (London, 1959), p. 39.
5 L. C. Knights, *An Approach to Hamlet* (London and Toronto, 1960), p. 59.
6 *Søren Kierkegaard's Journals and Papers*, vols. I–VI, ed. Howard V. Hong and Edna H. Hong (Bloomington and London, 1967–78), vol. III, entry 2344.
7 *Ibid.* vol. VI, entry 6903.
8 *Concluding Unscientific Postscript*, trans. L. M. Swenson and D. F. Lowrie (Princeton, 1974), pp. 105–6.
9 *Journals and Papers*, vol. II, entry 1578.
10 *Ibid.* vol. V, entry 5900.
11 From *Authority and Revelation*, p. 154, quoted in *Journals and Papers*, vol. II, p. 576.
12 *Either/Or*, trans. D. F. and L. M. Swenson (Princeton, 1971), vol. I, p. 153 (my italics).
13 *The Concept of Dread*, p. 39.
14 One might imagine that 'put on' meant something like 'given authority' or even 'made king'. But I use the phrase here in any or all the senses authorized for this particular line in Shakespeare by the *O.E.D.* ('to urge onward, encourage; to incite, impel'); by Caldecott in

Furness's *Variorum* edition ('put to the proof'); by the Arden edition ('brought to trial'); and Dover Wilson ('set to work'). Has not Hamlet been amply incited, put to the proof, brought to trial (shades of Kafka here!) and set to work?

15 For a discussion of the chronology of the plays see ch. 1 n. 16.
16 Macbeth says: 'To know my deed, 'twere best not know myself.' His tragedy is that he is forced to know both. Hamlet does not know either. This is the great objection to Nietzsche's view of the play (in *The Birth of Tragedy*), that Hamlet is paralysed by looking into the abyss of things and understanding too much: 'I do not know', says Hamlet. He understands nothing.

Chapter 8

1 *Diaries of Franz Kafka, 1910–1923*, ed. Max Brod (London, 1964).
2 *Edward Thomas, The Last Four Years* (Book I of the *Memoirs of Eleanor Farjeon*).
3 See Bailey, *Hamlet in France*; G. Wilson Knight, *Byron and Shakespeare* (London, 1966).
4 *The Trial*, trans. by Willa and Edwin Muir (New York, 1956), p. 4.
5 From a notebook published in *Wedding Preparations in the Country and Other Posthumous Prose Writings*, trans. by Ernst Kaiser and Eithne Wilkins (London, 1973).
6 'Letter to his Father', in *ibid.* pp. 205–6.
7 C. S. Lewis, 'Hamlet: The Prince or the Poem', in *Studies in Shakespeare*, ed. Peter Alexander (London, 1964).
8 Eleanor Prosser, *Hamlet and Revenge* (Stanford and London, 1967). See below, pp. 139, 144–5.
9 Hamlet's odd train of thought here was first pointed out to me by W. W. Robson.
10 I am indebted here to H. A. Mason's discussion of Act I of the play: see '"The Ghost in *Hamlet*"; A Resurrected "Paper"', *Cambridge Quarterly*, iii, 2 (1967–8).
11 E.g. by D. H. Lawrence, 'Introduction to these Paintings' (cf. above, pp. 85, 159).
12 The third Octavo notebook in the volume *Wedding Preparations in the Country*, pp. 83 and 48.
13 'The Judgement', in *The Penal Colony* (New York, 1964), p. 61.
14 *Wedding Preparations in the Country*, pp. 79–80.

Chapter 9

1 *Œuvres en Prose* (Paris, 1965), pp. 1455–6.
2 *Cahiers*, vol. ii (Paris, 1974), p. 1191.
3 This latter problem was pointed out to me by P. W. K. Stone. It could

just be that Ophelia is referring to the moment when, as she relates, Hamlet came to her closet and behaved like a distraught lover or madman. But his behaviour there does not quite seem like 'unkindness', and Ophelia virtually assents to Polonius's idea when he asks 'Mad for thy love?', rather than feels that Hamlet has turned against her at this point. Or, her pious couplet about unkind givers could be part of her instructions from Polonius: but that too does not quite fit, since the excuse would not be a good one in the circumstances; it would have been more apt to say something like 'It is improper for me to receive these gifts.' It remains a problem and another example of where evidence relating to an important issue is left out or withheld.

4 Hegel, *On Tragedy*, ed. A. and H. Paolucci (New York, 1975), pp. 294–5.
5 Ronald Gray, 'But Kafka Wrote in German', *Cambridge Quarterly*, VII, 3 (1977), pp. 211–12.

Part 2

1 C. S. Lewis, 'Hamlet: The Prince or the Poem?', in *Studies in Shakespeare*, ed. Peter Alexander (London, 1964).
2 Quotations from *Hamlet* are taken from the New American Library edition, ed. Edward Hubler (New York, Toronto and London, 1963).
3 Stoll, *'Hamlet': An Historical and Comparative Study* (Minneapolis, 1919); Dover Wilson, *What Happens in 'Hamlet'?* (Cambridge, 1935); Prosser, *Hamlet and Revenge*, pp. 119ff.
4 Santayana has some eloquent reflections on the ambiguous nature of the Ghost: 'It speaks, as Hamlet justly feels, by the ambiguous authority of heaven and hell at once...Ostensibly an emissary from the other world, such as would be admissible by a slightly heterodox Christian fancy, the Ghost is at the same time an echo of popular fable and demonology, and withal a moral and dramatic symbol, and definite *point d'appui* for the hero's morbid impulses' ('Hamlet', *Selected Critical Writings of George Santayana*, ed. N. Henfrey (Cambridge, 1968), vol. I, pp. 133–4).
5 See Mason, '"The Ghost in *Hamlet*": A Resurrected "Paper"' (see Ch. 8 n. 10). In this discussion of the Ghost I am indebted to Professor Mason's paper at several points.
6 Dover Wilson, *What Happens in 'Hamlet'*, pp. 78–86; Prosser, *Hamlet and Revenge*, pp. 139ff.
7 See, for example, Edward Dowden, *Shakespeare: His Mind and Art* (London, 1967).
8 See G. Wilson Knight, 'The Embassy of Death: An Essay on *Hamlet*', in *The Wheel of Fire* (London, 1969).
9 L. C. Knights, *An Approach to 'Hamlet'* (London and Toronto, 1960), p. 59.
10 Weston Babcock makes the interesting suggestion that Hamlet's

Notes for pages 149–186

disillusionment about his gifts to Ophelia ('I never gave you aught')
might also be prompted by the Ghost's account of Claudius's 'traitorous
gifts' to the Queen ('*Hamlet*': *A Tragedy of Errors* (Bloomington, 1967),
p. 59).

11 Middleton Murry, *Shakespeare* (London, 1936), pp. 237–8.
12 Samuel Johnson, *Prose and Poetry*, ed. Mona Wilson (London, 1963),
 pp. 614–15.
13 *A Portrait of the Artist as a Young Man* (Harmondsworth, 1975),
 Ch. III.
14 In *Cambridge Quarterly*, VI, 4 (1975). I am indebted to Professor
 Robson's article, and also (more broadly than can be adequately
 acknowledged here) to lectures and papers on *Hamlet* which he has
 given at the University of Oxford and elsewhere. His argument in the
 above article finally has implications for a view of the play as a whole.
 The question that he asks is: Did Shakespeare create a dramatic
 technique to give expression to a thought like Wittgenstein's, 'The
 world of the happy man is a different one from the world of the
 unhappy man'?
15 H. D. F. Kitto, *Form and Meaning in Drama* (London, 1959).
16 Prosser, *Hamlet and Revenge*, pp. 196–7.
17 John Lawlor, *The Tragic Sense in Shakespeare* (London, 1960), p. 66.
18 *Twilight in Italy*, p. 76.
19 T. S. Eliot, 'Hamlet', in *Selected Essays* (see Ch. 4 n. 3), p. 144; *Coleridge
 on Shakespeare*, ed. T. Hawkes (Harmondsworth, 1969), p. 90.
20 This is pointed out by M. M. Mahood, *Shakespeare's Wordplay* (London,
 1968), p. 128.
21 A. C. Bradley, *Shakespearian Tragedy* (London, 1971), p. 116.
22 Madariaga, *On Hamlet*, pp. 102–3.
23 Eliot, *Selected Essays*, p. 146.
24 Montaigne, II.xii, *An Apologie of Raymond Sebond*, in Florio's translation
 (London and Toronto, 1921), p. 139.
25 Tolstoy, 'Shakespeare and the Drama', *Recollections and Essays*, trans.
 A. Maude (London, 1937), p. 351. The critic had better beware of
 Tolstoy, who mocked the idea that 'in the person of Hamlet, a perfectly
 new and profound character is most powerfully presented; consisting
 in this, that the person has no character...' But one can reply, I think,
 that Tolstoy was antagonized particularly by those nineteenth-century
 German critics who made Shakespeare's 'creation of character' into
 the overriding reason for his superiority as a dramatist; that Tolstoy
 does not see Hamlet as unique in his lack of created and coherent
 'character', but simply as the most extreme manifestation of a fault
 found also in Lear, Othello and others (whereas I am arguing that this
 lack may to some extent be intended by Shakespeare, and sets Hamlet
 apart from the other tragic heroes); and finally that it may still be
 possible, particularly today, to see lack of 'identity' or the inability to
 realize the authentic 'self' as a legitimate subject for drama.

196

Index

Index

198

Index

Index

Tolstoy, Leo ('Shakespeare and the Drama'), 186, 196n.25

tradition, *see under* Eliot, *Hamlet*, Joyce, Mallarmé, Valéry; *see also* authority

Turgenyev, Ivan ('Hamlet and Don Quixote' and 'A Hamlet of the Schtigri District'), 8; on idealism in Hamlet, lack of, 8

Valéry, Paul, 6, 7, 33, 125, 130, 194n.2 (ch. 9)
'La Crise de l'Esprit', 33; interpretation of *Hamlet*, 125; on the Ghost in *Hamlet*, 33, 130; on tradition, 33, 130

Waldock, A. J. A. ('*Hamlet*': *A Study in Critical Method*), 160–1

Wilde, Oscar, 60

Wilson, Edmund (*Axel's Castle*), 60, 192n.3 (ch. 5)

Wilson, John Dover: edition of *Hamlet*, 170, 177, 183; *What Happens in 'Hamlet'?*, 139, 144–5, 158, 195nn.3, 6 (of Part 2)

Wittgenstein, Ludwig, 196n.14

Yeats, W. B., 8–9, 187n.3; on heroism of Hamlet, 8–9